AUTHORITY AND FREEDOM

SOME PSYCHOLOGICAL PROBLEMS
OF RELIGIOUS BELIEF

The Hulsean Lectures delivered at the
University of Cambridge, 1952

AUTHORITY
AND FREEDOM

SOME PSYCHOLOGICAL PROBLEMS
OF RELIGIOUS BELIEF

By

ROBERT H. THOULESS, Sc.D.

Fellow of Corpus Christi College, Cambridge
Reader in Educational Psychology in
the University of Cambridge

LONDON
HODDER AND STOUGHTON

FIRST PRINTED 1954

MADE AND PRINTED IN GREAT BRITAIN
FOR HODDER AND STOUGHTON LIMITED,
LONDON, BY T. AND A. CONSTABLE LTD.,
PRINTERS, EDINBURGH

PREFACE

I AM a psychologist, not a theologian; a layman, not a commissioned teacher in the Church. There are obvious disadvantages in one who is not a theologian venturing to discuss theological topics. They are the disadvantages of anyone who trespasses outside his own field of knowledge, that he may err through ignorance of a great deal of background knowledge which is taken for granted by the specialist in that field. I cannot hope that I have not erred in this way. On the other hand, there are some compensating advantages in the hope that one may be able to view the field from a different angle from that customary amongst specialists in it and may even be able to see different things in it. Being a layman has, I think, considerable advantages for the purpose that I have in mind. The layman has no responsibility for transmitting a tradition and may freely make suggestions without a fear that his suggestions will be treated as authoritative. He need not fear to make suggestions because they may be wrong; they will be treated as suggestions and not as authoritative pronouncements.

The governing principle of the psychological study of religion is generally recognised to be that called by Flournoy the principle of "exclusion of transcendence". By this principle the psychologist is limited to the description of the facts of the religious life without consideration of problems of reality or value. In these lectures I have disregarded this limitation and have so trespassed beyond the field of psychology. I have done this deliberately because the psychologist also is concerned with the practical problems which arise from his study, and is interested in asking not only about the nature of religious behaviour but also whether this is a rationally justified kind of behaviour and what ways of thinking, if any, provide justification for it.

I have here concerned myself with three main problems: first, is there now a decline in religious conviction? secondly, is it possible for a reasonable modern man to accept a religious system of thought? and thirdly, are there respects in which religious ideas are presented to the modern man which unnecessarily increase his difficulty of acceptance? I am suggesting an affirmative answer to all of these questions. With respect to the third, I suggest that one of the central difficulties is an overvaluation of doctrinal conformity. Since it seems generally to be supposed that any criticism of overemphasis on orthodoxy implies that the person making the criticism rejects orthodoxy, I wish to make it clear that I personally accept the Catholic tradition as handed down in the Church of England. I also accept the statement in the 19th Article of Religion: "As the Church of *Jerusalem*, *Alexandria*, and *Antioch*, have erred; so also the Church of *Rome* hath erred." This, I think, carries the implication that so also may the Church of England have erred, and I do not regard loyalty to the Church of England as requiring that her members should refrain from criticising her present position but rather that they should ask whether there are not changes in her doctrinal position which would more fully express her essential spirit.

I am grateful to the Rev. R. C. Walls for reading and criticising the first four chapters, and I regret that lack of time prevented me from having the benefit of his criticisms of the whole book.

I am also indebted to Sir Will Spens for reading the two chapters on authority, and in particular for criticisms of Chapter 7 which enabled me to remove some of its original imperfections. My debt to Sir Will Spens is indeed greater than this, since I have had discussions with him on related topics during the last forty years. Although I do not suppose he would agree with everything I have said, I feel sure that without his influence and encouragement this book would never have been written.

I am indebted to my wife for reading the typescript and proof and for removing many errors. It is hardly necessary to add that my debt to her in the making of the book also goes far beyond this.

R. H. THOULESS

2 LEYS ROAD, CAMBRIDGE
August 29, 1953

CONTENTS

Chapter One

THE DECLINE OF RELIGIOUS BELIEF

O NE of the most obvious practical problems in religion at the present day is the widespread falling away from religious belief. There are many suggested solutions of this problem. The religious modernist is inclined to say that the only hope of a return to religious belief is by the revision of our outworn dogmatic formulae and the restating of the Christian faith in terms of modern thought. The fundamentalists, on the other hand, invite us to turn away from the critical study of the Bible and to return to the idea that the Bible is the inspired Word of God literally true in all its parts. At the same time, we have the attitude towards the problem represented by Freud, who considers that this process is an inevitable result of the increased clear-sightedness of modern man, who is passing from childish trust in fairy stories which once consoled him and gave him motives for moral conduct to an adult state of scientific realisation of a Godless universe in which he must find rational grounds for morality when the irrational religious ones are discarded.[1]

Whatever may be its explanation, there seems little doubt of the reality of the falling away. The figures of church-membership in nearly all religious bodies in this country (with the exception, I believe, of the Roman Catholic Church) have shown a decline over many years. At one time I tried to make a rough esti-

[1] Freud, S., *The Future of an Illusion* (Eng. trans.), London, 1928.

mate of the extent of this decline by finding out from a group of extra-mural students at Glasgow University how their religious affiliations compared with those of their parents.[1] Of 110 people who answered my questions clearly enough to draw any conclusion, it appeared that about two-thirds were members of some religious organisation (about four-fifths of the women and rather less than three-fifths of the men). Only two out of the whole group were attached to a religious organisation although their parents had not been, but twenty-seven showed a change in the opposite direction, not being members of any religious body although their parents had been. The number investigated was too small for any very certain conclusion to be drawn, but the indications were of a net loss to religious organisations of about 23 per cent. in a single generation. This loss appeared to be greatest amongst the men (33 per cent. among the men and 16 per cent. among the women).

It may, of course, be objected that membership of a religious organisation is a superficial way of measuring religious faith, since many attached to religious organisations may have little religious conviction while some with no religious affiliations have strong religious beliefs. This is true, but, at the same time, religious affiliations are strongly correlated with religious convictions. They may, therefore, be used as a good but not perfect measure of religious conviction, and decline of church-membership is likely to be a fairly reliable indication of declining religious faith.

One must, however, remember that these results are valid only for the group and for the time at which they

---

[1] Thouless, R. H., "The changing character of organised religion: a study of the facts", *Hibbert Journal*, XXXIII, London, 1935.

were obtained. The enquiry took place in Scotland, and the figures of loss may be higher than they would have been in England because the process of decline may have started later in Scotland than in England. The date was 1935, and there are indications that the process has been to some extent reversed since then. I have no exact data for more recent times, but it is a general impression of those concerned with religious activities in the University of Cambridge that there is now a heightened interest in religion and a higher level of attendance at religious worship than there was before the 1939 war. I think this impression is probably correct. If it is, it is likely to be merely the reflection in one particular university of a change that is more widespread. However this may be, it remains true that the general level of religious faith is not high; a large part of the population of our country have little contact with religious thought and activity. Particularly we notice, in contrast with the situation a century ago, that a large proportion of the intelligent and educated members of the community are alienated from religion, which they are often inclined to regard as a childish activity of no interest to the grown man.

Some, at any rate, of the factors causing this decline started operating some time ago. Any short discussion of its history can hardly escape the danger of being sketchy and inadequate, but an attempt at such a discussion is justified by the consideration that an understanding of the modern problem must depend in part on an appreciation of the situation out of which it developed.

During the first half of the nineteenth century the general level of acceptance of the traditional religious attitudes was higher than it is at the present day. It is true that, even after the work of Wesley, there were large masses of people still outside the circle of influence of organised religion, but the majority of respectable and educated people were church-goers of unquestioning orthodoxy of belief. Much happened to religious belief during the nineteenth century. There was a rise of liberalism in religious thought which was strongly condemned by Newman in his *Apologia*.[1] The more conservative members of the churches particularly saw danger in the foundation of the Broad Church movement by Archbishop Whately, although Whately would certainly not seem dangerously unorthodox to any of us at the present time. At about the same time the Tractarian movement developed and left a lasting effect on the Church of England, although many of its leaders seceded to the Church of Rome.

These, however, were movements within fairly narrow limits of conventional orthodoxy. An event which seemed to threaten the foundations of accepted conventions of orthodoxy was the publication in 1859 of Darwin's *Origin of Species*.[2] After that, the pattern of Victorian orthodoxy never completely recovered its stability. Looking back at it now, the disturbance over Darwin's ideas may seem to us to be a storm in a teacup. If, however, we realise the religious presuppositions of the time at which it appeared, we can see that there was reason for concern. The main thing that troubled Darwin's contemporaries seems unimportant to us now, that his theory implied that the creation of organic life took place otherwise than as reported in the Book of Genesis. It seemed, therefore, that if Darwin

[1] Newman, J. H., *Apologia pro Vita Sua*, London, 1864.
[2] Darwin, C. R., *The Origin of Species by means of Natural Selection*, London, 1859.

was right, the Bible was not true; it was, at any rate,
clear that the Biblical narrative was not true in the
sense in which contemporary religious thinkers had
supposed it to be true.

There was good reason for the contradiction of the
creation account in Genesis having seemed more important a hundred years ago than it would to us at the
present time. It is true that the literal truth of all parts
of the Bible was not stated anywhere in the formulation
of doctrine required to be believed, at any rate by the
Church of England. The sixth of the Articles of Religion
said: "Holy Scripture containeth all things necessary
to salvation", but this neither states nor logically implies
that all things contained in the accepted version of the
Scriptures must be taken as literally true. There is no
reasonable doubt that the authors of the Articles of
Religion believed in the literal accuracy of the Bible
since this is an implication of the practice common to
Catholics and Protestants alike at the time of the
Reformation of appealing to isolated texts of Scripture
to support disputed points of doctrine. But the implied
theory of the inerrancy of all Scripture was not stated;
Darwin's account of the creation of living forms did not
contradict any explicit teaching of the Church.

It did, however, contradict what Darwin's contemporaries felt to be an essential part of the foundation of
Christian belief. Partly, no doubt, this feeling of the
necessity for a belief in the inerrancy of the Biblical
narrative arose from the tendency of the Reformation
to throw increased weight on the authority of Scripture.
Before the Reformation, the religious thinker would
have felt that his belief rested on the authority of the
Church and the Bible; some of the more radical of the
reformers would regard it as based on the authority of

the Divine Light in the individual believer. The general tendency of the Reformed Churches was, however, to base all authority on Scripture, and the suggestion that the Bible was not necessarily accurate in its accounts of facts seemed a dangerous threat to that authority. Obviously there was a need for the question of authority to be thought out afresh. It was natural, however, that the immediate reaction in the 1850s was to avoid this necessity by denying the fact of error in the first chapters of Genesis. That is psychologically understandable, if it is intellectually unsound.

It was in a sense only a historical accident that this necessity for a revaluation of the authority of Scripture made its first impact on religious thought as a result of Darwin's work. The same necessity was presented in a more drastic form by the results of critical study of the Bible. This study had already started before the publication of the *Origin of Species*, although general recognition of its significance came later. A hundred years earlier, Anstruc had taken the first step by pointing out that the Genesis account of creation was compiled from two sources which were not altogether consistent with one another. It was not, however, until in 1864 Bishop Colenso was censured by Convocation for questioning the Mosaic authorship of the Pentateuch and the historical accuracy of the early books of the Bible that there was general recognition of the fact that something was happening here also that threatened the general assumption of the verbal accuracy of the Bible. Again the first reaction was one of shocked repudiation, but Biblical study went on and it became increasingly difficult to ignore its results.

It must be borne in mind that, although Biblical criticism was mainly the work of scholars and decisions on many critical points could only be made by those who had good knowledge of Greek or Hebrew, the main points that bear on the question of verbal inerrancy need for their understanding no knowledge of ancient tongues and can be verified as well by the man in the street as by the scholar. The fact that there are in the Book of Genesis two accounts of the Creation which are not in complete agreement, that there are also two accounts of the Flood which differ on various points, that the different Gospels differ in the chronology of Our Lord's life, in the exact words he used, in the date of the crucifixion and in their account of the events leading up to it—all of this can be discovered by anyone comparing different parts of his Bible with careful attention without knowledge of any other language than his own. And what he can so discover is plainly inconsistent with that literal truth of the Bible which Darwin's work was felt to challenge.

There was, however, a further and in some ways more serious result of the impact of Darwinism on religious belief. This was the apparent conflict between the scientific proposition that organic life had been developed by a blind process of weeding out the unfit forms of life, and the religious proposition that organic life was made by God (whether by a process of sudden creation or of continuous evolution). This seemed to be one more demonstration that religious belief was "unscientific", that the propositions on which it was based were in contradiction with proved scientific propositions. If, of course, the religious statement is treated as if it were a scientific statement, that is, as an alternative explanation of how organic life came into being, then there would be a contradiction and one would have to decide between the two statements by con-

B

sidering which is best supported by the available evidence. But this would be to misunderstand the character of religious statements; if we consider that these belong to a way of using language different from that of scientific description, then there is no contradiction between the two set of statements. They are simply saying different things about the coming into being of organic life; both may be true.

The conflict which is real is not between the statements of science and of religion but between those of religion and of scientific naturalism. We can use the term "scientific naturalism" for the view that would have been once expressed as that the world of physical objects and their interrelations studied by science is the only reality; a more modern statement of this view would be that the only significant statements are the descriptive and explanatory statements about these physical objects which make up the system of the sciences (including natural history, behaviouristic psychology, and the social sciences). Between the view of scientific naturalism and religion there is an irreconcilable conflict; one cannot both assert that nothing more is to be said about the origin of life than is said by evolutionary biology and also that life was made by God.

If this is admitted, it places the difference between the religious and the scientific systems of thought elsewhere than it appeared in the last century. Most of those who now defend the religious system of thought would agree that its acceptance must not be regarded as entailing the denial of any scientific assertion. It does involve the denial of the further assertion which may be made on behalf of science that its true assertions are all the assertions that can be significantly made. Nor does the acceptance of the religious point of view entail that of possible scientific assertions some are to be chosen rather than others, e.g. the biological theories of vitalism rather than those of mechanism. For a vitalistic biologist might make the assertion that what is said about life on his theory is all that can significantly be said, while a mechanistic biologist might not make this further assertion. The former denies the possibility of religious propositions in connection with life while the latter does not. Which is the more adequate theory must, of course, be decided on scientific grounds; neither is to be regarded as in any sense preferable on religious grounds.

The above is obviously not an exhaustive account of the factors which led to a decline in religious faith. Those mentioned were, I think, the main starting-point of the idea that religious teachings were essentially irrational and in conflict with the proved results of science. There were other factors in the situation which also played a part in the decline of faith which were not connected with religious doctrines. There was, for example, the tendency to worldliness in the churches, as exemplified by the practice of seating the more prosperous members of the congregations in rented pews, while those who could not afford pew rents were seated relatively uncomfortably in less-honoured parts of the building. A secondary consequence of this worldliness was a lack of interest in social and industrial problems, leading to a tendency for humanitarian movements to be largely directed by those indifferent to religion or openly hostile to it. There were honourable exceptions to this rule, but it was sufficiently common to have directed away from the religious tradition many of those whose active love for their fellow-men might have predisposed them to religious activity if they had lived in the days of St. Francis or of St. Vincent de Paul.

The problems of belief which arose in the middle of the last century are by no means of merely historical interest. The idea that the solution of our present religious difficulties is to go back to the simple faith of our great-grandfathers is one that appeals to many people. The eloquent evangelist who proclaims that we must ignore the higher critics, repudiate Darwin, and return to the belief in the literal truth of the Bible can still persuade people that this is the one sure road to religious faith. We cannot follow him, because such a faith could only be accepted at the cost of sacrificing our intellectual integrity. And we ought not to wish to follow him, because he is pointing to a road that only goes back to a religious position fundamentally unstable. Impressive as was the façade of mid-nineteenth-century religion, its foundations were weak. It was because of that weakness that the system was so badly shaken by its exposure to the facts both of biological science and of Biblical criticism. A religion for the twentieth century must be built on firmer foundations.

Even if we could be content that simple and unlearned people should accept a "fundamentalist" faith which is at variance with the facts, knowing that those who accept it might never have their faith disturbed since they may never become aware of the facts which make their form of religious belief untenable, there would still remain another aspect to be considered. There is the case of the less simple person who supposes that the choice which lies before him is between a "fundamentalist" religion and no religion at all; who knows that the fundamentalist position is untenable and therefore chooses the alternative of no religion. If the Christian faith is to be made accessible to him, it must be by making clear to him that the choice is not as he supposes.

In all of this discussion we must, I think, bear in mind the needs both of the simple and unlearned and of the educated and enquiring. There has been a general tendency for liberal religious thinkers to over-estimate the importance of the educated and enquiring members of the Christian community at the expense of the simple and unlearned, while there has been a corresponding tendency for conservative religious thinkers to pay too little attention to the needs of the educated and enquiring in comparison with those of the simple and unlearned. Whether our own religious thought is inclined to be liberal or conservative, we must remember the needs of both groups. The way of simple trust and the way of intellectual enquiry are both ways to God. Neither is to be exalted at the expense of the other.

When I speak here of the educated and enquiring, I do not mean theologians and philosophers; I mean the ordinary man who is beginning to ask questions about his religion, who is not content to accept what his religious teachers tell him but is beginning to ask how he knows that what they say is true. Indeed, the individual who accepts his faith in simple trust and the one who criticises and enquires may not be different people. They may be the same individual at different stages of his life. Very often one who accepted in simple trust what he was taught about religion begins to en-quire and to read books of a sceptical or rationalistic tendency. Too often he thinks that this is a sign that he is losing his religious faith and that he is giving way to a sinful spirit of scepticism. It is very likely that his religious advisers and the implications of his early religious training encourage him in this view. So he may come to feel that the necessary consequence of his new outlook is that he must give up his religious practices, and he ceases to pray or to receive the Sacrament of Communion. There may be no one to tell him that there is nothing sinful about the attitude of scepticism or about intellectual enquiry in matters religious: that this also is a road to God, that it may indeed be the road which he has to travel now, and that to abandon it might be to turn his back on the type of activity that the Holy Spirit requires of him now.

On the social consequences of the decline of religious faith we have little precise information, but there is a widespread impression that they are on the whole undesirable. Personality maladjustments such as neurosis and delinquency are widespread. We do not know with certainty that they are increasing, but there is some reason for thinking that they may be and that one of the reasons for this is the absence of adequate motivation for the acceptance of frustration and for the carrying out of socialised behaviour.

One of the baffling problems in the psychological treatment of delinquency is that the delinquent seems generally to have no system of motivation that can be appealed to as a rational ground for living as a co-operative member of society instead of breaking into houses, assaulting women with handbags, and so on. It is often said that society must provide a system of motives by severe punishment; the delinquent must learn that crime does not pay. The trouble with this remedy is that it does not go deep enough; that he should do what pays and avoid what does not pay is a lesson that the delinquent may find it easy to learn while remaining at heart a delinquent. He may at best become what Aichorn has called a "latent delinquent"[1] instead of an overt delinquent; he has not then become a good citizen. A better solution would be that he should adopt an attitude of regarding himself as a servant of God, of whose service an essential part is the love of one's neighbour.

It is true that this is not the only possible solution. It is also possible that he might learn to emancipate himself from the system of motivation provided by religion and to substitute for it a rational system of motivation for socialised behaviour based on a scientific (i.e. naturalistic) view of the world. This is certainly possible, as is shown by many upright unbelievers of high integrity, but the required substitution very commonly does not take place. The essential problem of juvenile delinquency is that many of the young people of the present day carry out the first step in this programme without carrying out the second; they reject the religious system of ideas but find no substitute system of motivation for socialised behaviour.

In many respects the problem of neurosis is parallel. Human life necessarily brings many frustrations both in the field of love and in the region of their self-esteem. A man or woman may react to these frustrations by compensatory processes such as developing a neurotic illness or by developing ideas of grandeur and of persecution, or by suicide. None of these reactions would seem to be reasonable to the man who accepted the religious point of view. If he considers himself primarily as an instrument of the Divine will, he cannot much resent frustration even of what he feels to be

[1] Aichorn, A., *Wayward Youth* (Eng. trans.), London, 1936.

his deepest needs. Loss can then be accepted cheerfully if it is felt that it is not the will of God that he should have what he seems to need. If he experiences failure or lack of recognition, these will not seem important to him if he is convinced that the purpose of the world is to promote the glory of God and not his own personal ends. He is thus armed against the refusal to accept frustration and against feeling resentment at humiliation. He has an adequate system of motivation for accepting these things instead of reacting against them by personality disturbances of a neurotic kind.

It is true that religious ideas may be found amongst neurotic persons and even amongst the insane, and may indeed be an essential ingredient of the neurotic or insane system of ideas. Thus an obsessional patient may have a compulsion to carry out a religious act, such as to cross himself or to make an act of the presence of God every time the clock strikes the hour, and he may suffer from neurotic anxiety if he has accidentally omitted to carry out these compulsive acts. A depressed patient may suffer from an overwhelming sense of guilt because he believes that he has committed the unforgivable sin. It is possible to interpret such facts as evidence that the possession of a religious system of ideas may render an individual prone to neurosis or to some forms of insanity. They may, however, have another explanation. An obsessional neurotic or a melancholic patient may simply be inclined to twist any system of ideas that is available to him in such a way that it serves the ends of his illness. In all such cases, there is a distortion of religious ideas, since in both the set of religious ideas connected with the guilt of sin is disconnected from the set of religious ideas connected with repentance and forgiveness. The recovery of mental health may not be by the turning of the patient away from his religious ideas, but by leading him through these to a more balanced attitude in which he accepts the whole of the religious system of ideas and not only a part of it.

If, however, we agree that the provision of motives for good citizenship and for the acceptance of frustration are psychological consequences of religious faith, it does not follow that they can properly be regarded as primary objects of religious faith. We may be tempted to teach religion to delinquents in approved schools in order to make them better citizens, or to encourage the neurotic to accept a religious system of belief as a means to mental health. But this is to treat religion as a means and not as itself an end. "God" is not the name of a conceptual device for securing good citizenship and mental health. It is an offence against intellectual honesty to teach a system of ideas not because we think they are true but because we think they may be useful to the people to whom we teach them.

It may, indeed, be one reason for the common falling away from religious faith in late adolescence that religion is often taught to children as a means to secure good behaviour. In an unpublished essay on *The Genesis of non-Belief*, by Jahoda, it is noted that a large number of unbelievers send their children to Sunday school and to church because they think that the acquiring of religious ideas will make them better citizens. It is not only amongst unbelievers that one finds the idea that the giving of supernatural motives to children may be a convenient way of getting them to behave in the ways required by adults. I remember a sermon for children which I once heard by a leading divine of the Church of Scotland. It was on "The voice of God", and its theme was that the children often did not do the things which the voice of God told them to do. I recollect two of the items which the preacher said were the injunctions of the voice of God. One was "Don't slam the door" and the other was "Don't contradict your parents". I do not think it would need a very intelligent child to suspect that what the preacher called "the voice of God" was what he had already learned to recognise as the voice of his parents but given an imaginative celestial setting. That suspicion might well be dangerous to the child's developing religious faith. Adults take a very grave responsibility when they use religious ideas as a means of securing their own convenience. They may for a time succeed in imposing a religious sanction for their own requirements, but critical reflection is liable to start at about the time of adolescence. The adolescent will find little foundation for building an adult religious faith on a system of early teaching which he has reason to believe was not about something that governed his parents' own beliefs and conduct but rather a system of fairy-tales told to children to make them good.

A well-founded faith must be one that is regarded as an end and not as a means. Not that men should believe that there is a God because that belief will give them a system of motives for good citizenship, that they should cultivate a love for God because this will console them for deprivations in their love life on earth, or that they should think of themselves as God's servants because they will then be protected against shocks to their self-esteem. The right reason for believing in God is that this alone embodies a correct opinion about the universe and our own place in it; the right reason for loving and serving him is that it was for this end we were created. To a faith so founded on a conviction of reality, such other gifts as good citizenship and mental stability may be added as secondary consequences. They must not themselves be regarded as primary ends to be achieved through religious faith.

Chapter Two

IS DOGMA AN OBSTACLE TO FAITH?

ONE of the causes that has been suggested for the decline of religious faith is that acceptance of religious faith involves also the acceptance of a system of dogmas which the modern man finds himself unable to believe. It is clear that any religious body must carefully consider what doctrines it requires its members to believe as a condition of their membership, although it may be thought that in the past these doctrinal requirements have been too rigid. What is untrue or uncertain must be discarded; much that is true need not be regarded as essential. But the questions to be asked are those of truth and value, not of acceptability to the modern mind; the modern mind may be wrong.

In the study by Jahoda already mentioned, the reasons given for rejection of the Christian faith by unbelievers were not generally intellectual but more commonly social and emotional; for example, "Religious people are hypocrites" and "I have just lost interest in the whole thing". Less commonly an intellectual reason was given, such as: "Christianity fails to recognise the inherent weakness of human nature" and "Religion is unscientific".[1]

When intellectual reasons are given, it would be naïve to accept these at their face value. Neither in rejecting nor in accepting religious faith are people likely to be swayed primarily by intellectual considera-

[1] Jahoda, G., *The Genesis of non-Belief* (unpublished).

tions. Intellectual reasons for or against are very often likely to be to some extent "rationalisations": intellectual covers for attitudes adopted on emotional grounds. At the same time, intellectual considerations do, no doubt, play their part in determining belief. It is important that the doctrinal requirements of religious bodies should not place unnecessary obstacles in the way of the acceptance of their faith.

Radical religious reformers sometimes recommend a general rejection of traditional dogma on the ground that the modern mind refuses to be "fettered by outworn creeds". Whether or not some reform is necessary in connection with dogma, we can only muddle ourselves by thinking in inappropriate metaphors. It is unpleasant to think of ourselves as fettered, and there may be attitudes towards dogma which make it unnecessarily fettering to thought, but the essence of a doctrinal system is simply that a system of assertions is accepted and believed. Any assertion, whether religious or secular, limits the freedom of the person making the assertion also to make other assertions which are incompatible with it. A man may make the positive assertion "I believe P", or the negative assertion "I disbelieve P", or the agnostic assertion "I do not know whether P is true or false". Whichever he asserts, he has so far fettered himself that he is not then free to make either of the other assertions about P. In this sense, he is no less fettered if he makes the agnostic statement than if he makes either of the other two. This is the case whether P stands for "the existence of God" or "the virgin birth of Jesus Christ" or "the bodily assumption of the Blessed Virgin Mary". Our choice as to whether to assert or deny any of these dogmas must obviously depend on whether we have sound reasons for thinking that they are true, and not on fear of being fettered by a positive assertion.

This metaphor is also objectionable in the implications of the word 'outworn'. Some things (such as knives and other physical implements) become increasingly unserviceable as they grow older; other things (such as the multiplication table) do not. There is no necessity for supposing that dogmas belong to the first class rather than to the second. If a true assertion was made many centuries ago, there is no gain in replacing it by a false statement made more recently. No reverence for antiquity must make us hesitate to discard an old statement if we have good reason for thinking that it is false. But the question is one of truth or falsity, not of age as is implied by the use of the word 'outworn'.

A less radical solution of the practical problem of the obstacle that a modern man may find in the doctrinal system of a Church that he is disposed to join is that this should be restated in terms of modern thought. While one may feel sympathetic with this proposal, it is necessary to ask whether the difficulty about religious dogma is to be found to any considerable extent in its out-of-date language and the unfamiliar modes of thinking it embodies, and whether, so far as that is a difficulty, it is to be removed by any process of translation into modern terms.

Clearly to understand the doctrines of religion, one must be prepared to use the language in which they are stated. To treat as literal description what is metaphorical (or symbolic) is to misunderstand religious dogma basically, and it will then appear a great obstacle to the intellectually alert modern man. But this difficulty is not to be overcome by putting religious dogma into terms of modern thought. A modern metaphor is as misleading as an ancient one if the reader does not understand its metaphorical nature and the rules of use of metaphorical language.

It is true, of course, that language changes and that doctrines couched in the language of the sixteenth century may be misunderstood by those who understand only the way in which language is used in the twentieth century. The word 'substance', for example, as used in the Nicene and Athanasian Creeds is likely to be understood in a sense very different from that in which it was used, as "matter" rather than as "essence", so that such a phrase as "of one substance with his Father" may suggest a meaning extremely different from that intended. The opening phrase of the Athanasian Creed: "Whosoever will be saved . . ." seems to the modern reader to mean "Whoever is going to be saved . . . " and not, as it did to the original translators, "Whoever wants to be saved. . . ." These are real inconveniences, inseparable from the use of a living language for formulating the creeds. These can only continue to be correctly understood if the words used in their formulation are frequently changed as these words change their meanings in current speech; a time-lag of four centuries is too long if we are to avoid misunderstandings.

One can, of course, escape this inconvenience by retaining the creeds in a dead language which is, as it were, a technical vocabulary the meaning of whose terms is fixed by definition and is, therefore, not subject to the fluctuations of meaning in ordinary speech. This also has inconveniences. The reformers made the choice of translating the creeds into the vulgar tongue without also making any provision for keeping the translation changed as the usages of ordinary speech changed. This was a mistake, natural perhaps at the time, but we have no good excuse for perpetuating the mistake.

This, however, is only a relatively superficial aspect of the problem of restating the doctrines of the Church in terms of modern thought. Those who use this phrase mean much more than changing the words of the doctrines in such a way that the meanings are kept constant. Their complaint is rather that religious dogmas embody a way of thinking which is no longer a current way of thinking, and that they need to be restated in terms of contemporary thought.

While admitting that the philosophy of the first few centuries of Christianity is not one used currently in other contexts, we need not fall into the error of underestimating the intellectual acumen of the early theologians. The late Archbishop Temple, for example, wrote in *Foundations*: "These writers [the early theologians] had very little grasp of personal individuality; they did not see clearly that because I am I, I cannot be anyone else."[1] With all reverence for the opinion of Archbishop Temple, I find it difficult to believe that a proposition that would seem obvious to a modern schoolboy would not also have appeared obvious to St. Athanasius and his contemporaries. I suggest that they did understand this but that they also understood that the logic of ways of talking about ordinary human personalities might not be appropriate to the problems of the Godhead. I do not think that the makers of our creeds suffered from any lack of intellectual clarity; it is rather to be supposed that what they did was as well done as it could have been done either then or now.

[1] Temple, W., "The Divinity of Christ", *Foundations*, London, 1913.

This is not to say that we have no advantages in considering their problems. We have seen the rise and fall of many philosophies and can take a comparative view of philosophical systems. We can regard a philosophy as a language system in which what can be said is to some extent dictated by the system adopted. We are no longer tempted to regard an expression of an idea in a particular philosophical language as the one way in which that idea can be correctly expressed. We look rather on the restatement of an old idea in the terms of a new philosophy as a kind of translation, and we are interested in such questions as that of the nature of a language system in which religious ideas can be expressed and its relation to other language systems.

There is no doubt that theologians always will try to restate the doctrines of the Christian Church in modern terms, and this intellectual activity is a defensible one although it is perhaps less important than those who carry it out may be inclined to suppose. Its justification is the same as that of any theoretical intellectual activity, as, for example, scientific theorising or the original activities of the makers of creeds. It is true that, in historical fact, statements of orthodox doctrine have generally been formulated in order to exclude views that the Church regarded as heretical, but the whole intellectual activity of making heresies and making creeds can be regarded as a typical expression of a deep-seated psychological tendency to try to impose order on our experiences by making theories about them.

The devout man, impatient of theologies, may object that one can love God and serve him without considering whether the Trinity is to be thought of as three persons, or as three substances, or as three aspects of the Godhead. This is obviously true, but the situation is not very different in scientific theorising. Psychologists have spent much time in discussing whether we perceive things as wholes or whether perception is the integration of atomic sensations. The plain man could object that the actual business of perceiving can be carried out just as efficiently whichever of these theories one holds or if one has no theory on the matter at all. This also is obviously true, but the psychologist has two lines of justification for his interest in the theoretical question. First, as a psychologist he feels that it is his intellectual duty to think rightly on the question whether it has any practical implications or not. Secondly, he may say that, although holding the correct theory on the matter does not make his perception of the external world any more efficient than that of the man in the street, it does affect the solution of other problems of practice, such as, for example, what techniques of painting will give a good representation of objects depicted, or what kind of display on a switchboard will lead to the most efficient operating.

The theologian, trying to construct a theory of the Nature of the Trinity or of the Incarnation has the same justification. He may feel that it is his intellectual duty to get the matter straight, and he may rightly consider that its solution does affect practical problems of religious devotion even though it is obviously true that the basic religious attitudes of love and service are possible with various solutions of the theoretical problems or with none at all. These justifications are valid for the early theologians constructing the creeds or for Professor Sanday putting forward the more modern theory that the seat of divinity in Jesus Christ was his subconscious.[1]

[1] Sanday, W., *Christologies Ancient and Modern*, Oxford, 1910.

If these are the justifications for theologising, it is a proper exercise of the human intellect, although a less important one than has been traditionally supposed. We can accept neither the view that the traditional solutions of theoretical problems of theology are theories which must be believed as a condition of salvation, nor that it is necessary for the modern Christian to be aware of the speculations of modern theologians. When a modern writer of a popular book on the Christological problem claims it as the purpose of his book to arouse its readers from their "dogmatic slumbers",[1] I think it is reasonable to suggest that he is overvaluing theological speculation. The theologian perhaps ought to grapple with theological problems; there seems no reason for thinking that it is of any advantage to the ordinary Christian believer that he should do so. Is he not more likely to develop his religious life if he engages in prayer and in works of charity than if he speculates on whether the seat of Divinity in Jesus Christ was the subconscious or if he considers the doctrine of the Incarnation in the "fresh light which has come from the psychoanalysts and from psychical research"?[1]

In his letters to Bishop Serapion concerning the Holy Spirit, St. Athanasius made it clear that he did not regard speculations of this order as normal Christian activities, and lack of interest in theological speculation as a state analogous to slumber. On the contrary, after discussing whether the Spirit was begotten by the Father, he said: "Nor is it fitting to ask such questions about the Godhead. For God is not as man, that we should dare to ask human questions about Him. We

---

[1] Matthews, W. R., *The Problem of Christ in the Twentieth Century*, London, 1950.

ought, therefore . . . to be silent on these matters and to disregard these people. But, lest our silence should furnish an excuse for their effrontery, let them listen."[1]

One may indeed consider that a purpose served by official formulations of doctrine is that they enable the ordinary Christian believer to carry on the Christian life without concerning himself with theoretical speculations. I think this is a real advantage, although sometimes it has been attained at too high a price in intellectual freedom. There seems, however, to be no reason for trying to lead the ordinary (non-theological) Christian believer to think that he has a duty of engaging in theological speculation.

It is in the light of our opinion as to the value of theologising that one must consider the programme of restating the Christian doctrines in modern terms. Three points may be considered in respect to this programme. First, are the traditional formulations so unintelligible as we are led to believe? Secondly, would a reformulation in modern terms make them intelligible? Thirdly, would it achieve the aim of freeing the Christian believer from dogmatic fetters? It is not my intention to argue that there is nothing we have to do about the doctrinal formulations of traditional Christianity, but that the idea of reformulation in modern terms is a diversion from the real problem which seems to me to be psychological rather than theological, a question of attitude towards dogma rather than of how to formulate it.

First, as to intelligibility of the traditional formulations, it may be that the difficulties of understanding appear more formidable to philosophers and theologians

---

[1] Athanasius, *The Letters of St. Athanasius concerning the Holy Spirit* (trans. C. R. B. Shapland), London, 1951.

than they do to the simple believer. If the traditional doctrines do not use the language of contemporary philosophy, the way of thinking that they embody may be nearer to ordinary popular thinking than is most contemporary philosophy. I am reminded of a true story which is, I think, illuminating on this question of intelligibility. A little girl of about eight was found in tears in bed by her mother. When asked what she was crying about, she replied that it was because she couldn't understand the doctrine of the Trinity. Her mother tried to explain the matter to her in simple words suitable for a child, but her tears continued to flow. Finally her mother said that she would read her something which was said by very wise men in the past, which she could not hope to understand now but which she might understand when she was older. She then got a prayer-book and read aloud the Athanasian Creed. As she listened to its sonorous and beautiful phrases the child's tears stopped. When her mother had finished the child said: "Oh, Mummy, why didn't you tell me that before; it makes everything quite clear."

As to why everything was then quite clear, I think the answer must be a psychological one. Any explanation seems perfectly clear if it fully relieves the state of tension which led to the demand for explanation and if no further difficulties are seen by the person to whom the explanation was given. It is not necessary also that the explanation should be perfectly clear in the logical sense that no further difficulties can possibly be raised. Nor is it necessary that an explanation which seems perfectly clear to a young child would appear so to a theologian or to a philosopher. He may see many further difficulties that the child does not see. But in evaluating the intelligibility of the ancient doctrinal formulations it must be considered that they may perform the function of removing difficulties for the simple and uninstructed even though they may appear full of difficulties to the learned.

Secondly, we must consider the value of reformulation in modern terms. This is often suggested as if it were a means of making the ancient teachings of the Church both intelligible and intellectually serviceable to the modern man. But when one considers in detail what is involved in this, there seem to be grave reasons for doubting both its practicability and its usefulness. An obvious difficulty which would face philosophers if they were asked to restate the creeds in terms of modern thought is that there is no common philosophical language which is "modern thought". This is one of the differences between the philosophical situation of the last three centuries and earlier times. Moreover, some of the philosophical languages available (such as those of scientific naturalism and logical positivism) follow a system of rules which exclude the possibility of stating a religious proposition. A Christian philosopher will, of course, try to state his faith in the terms of his own philosophy, and it will then be intelligible to those who accept that philosophy. It will not be generally intelligible. Anyone who wishes to understand a doctrinal statement must learn the terms used and the rules of its language. This necessity exists at present; it would exist no less if religious propositions were stated in terms of a current philosophy. For the ordinary Christian, the obstacle to understanding is likely to be greater in the second case than in the first.

It may, indeed, be necessary to accomplish a philosophical task more ambitious than that of translating the ancient terms into the language of a current philosophy. Modern religious philosophers may feel that their task is to create a philosophical terminology and rules for its use more adequate to the stating of religious propositions than any at present available.[1] Success in such an enterprise might be of great value as enabling one to put more clearly the points of difference in religious issues and providing a technique for deciding between more and less adequate ways of formulating religious propositions. It would not, however, provide a formulation intelligible to ordinary worshippers. Theologians might have to master the rules of its logic for their own purposes; it would not provide an easy road to making the Christian doctrines intelligible and acceptable to the average modern man.

Finally, a most serious objection to regarding as the most important immediate objective the reformulation of religious dogma in terms of modern thought is that such a reformulation does nothing to solve the real difficulty expressed in the phrase "fettered by outworn creeds". The important point is not the implication of the word 'outworn' but that of the word 'fettered'. If the demand for acceptance of the Christian creeds is felt to be a fetter, more is required than that they should be restated in modern terms. One cannot achieve liberation merely by replacing ancient fetters by others of a more modern design. Must one not rather consider whether the attitude towards dogma needs revision?

[1] Masterman, Margaret, " Linguistic Philosophy, and Dogmatic Theology", *Theology*, LIV, London, 1951.

Chapter Three

PERSECUTION AND INTOLERANCE

THE necessity for a revision of traditional attitudes towards religious dogma is at no time brought home more forcibly to us than when we consider the facts of religious intolerance, particularly those of religious persecution. To get a fair picture of the facts of persecution and their bearing on the traditional attitude towards dogma, it is necessary that we should rid our minds of the tendency to escape from any sense of guilt about religious persecution by the use of the process which has been called by the psychoanalysts "projection", that is, by attributing persecution to those branches of the Christian Church with which we are not in agreement. Protestants have condemned Roman Catholic persecution, and Roman Catholics have condemned persecution of Roman Catholics by Protestants. In truth, both sides were guilty. Those of us who are members of the Church of England will profit little by deploring the burning of heretics under Queen Mary. It may be of some profit to us to remind ourselves of the burnings for heresy by the reformed English Church both before and after Queen Mary's reign.

After the breach with Rome in Henry VIII's reign, there were burnings both for the heresy of holding that the Pope was the Head of the Church (as John Forest in 1535) and in much greater number for the heresy of denying the doctrine of transubstantiation (as Anne Askew in 1546). Only two burnings for heresy took place in the reign of Edward VI. One of these was of Joan Bocher, who was burned in 1550 for the heresy of denying that our Lord took flesh of the Virgin Mary and who reproached her judges for having burned Anne Askew for a piece of bread although they had soon afterwards come themselves to believe and profess the same opinion for which they had burned her.[1]

In the reign of Elizabeth I, many Roman Catholic clergy were hanged for ministering to their co-religionists in England. At the same time there were also burnings for heresy. So late as the thirtieth year of her reign, Francis Kett, who appears to have been a former Fellow of my own College of Corpus Christi, Cambridge, was burned in the ditch of Norwich Castle by order of the Bishop of Norwich for holding "divers detestable opinions against Christ our Saviour".[2]

The exact nature of the opinions for which Kett suffered death is not, so far as I can discover, recorded. They may have been erroneous; it is possible also that they were detestable. He may have been worthy of blame and even deserving of punishment for teaching opinions contrary to the traditions of the Church of which he was an ordained minister. But, whatever his opinions were, they cannot have been so detestable as the implied opinion of his persecutors that they were carrying out the teaching of Jesus Christ by burning one who held or taught mistaken ideas about his person. That was a detestable and horrible error, compared with which any error in Kett's teaching must be regarded as relatively unimportant. Anne Askew,

[1] Gairdner, J., *Lollardy and the Reformation* (4 vols.), London, 1908.
[2] Masters, R., *The History of the College of Corpus Christi and the Blessed Virgin Mary*, Cambridge, 1753.

when warned by Bishop Gardiner that persistence in her denial of transubstantiation would put her in danger of the stake, replied very sensibly that she had searched all the Scriptures, yet she could never find that either Christ or his apostles put any creature to death.[1]

The Church of England was not, of course, alone guilty among the reformed Churches in this matter. Luther and Calvin burned heretics, as did the Inquisition. The theory behind persecution, that any means were justified to secure uniformity of belief, was not rejected by the reformers. It did not, in fact, succeed in securing its object, and persecution of heretics was gradually abandoned by all Churches. The death penalty for heresy lasted longest in Spain, where in 1826 a schoolmaster of blameless life was hanged for Deism, the last victim of the Spanish Inquisition.[2]

We are all now agreed in condemning persecution for heresy, and a consideration of persecution may seem to have no present-day importance. I suggest that it has, because the burning of heretics was so obviously and terribly wrong that we are driven to ask whether there was not something basically wrong with the presuppositions that led up to it. Athanasius and the other early theologians would, no doubt, have been horrified if they had seen the fires of Smithfield and of the Spanish Inquisition, but they may be regarded as having played some part in sowing the seed which produced this terrible harvest. We may consider that the seed itself is suspect, and we must question the whole attitude towards religious doctrine that led to such a perversion of the teaching of Christ. If we are

[1] Gairdner, J., *Lollardy and the Reformation* (4 vols.), London, 1908.
[2] Turberville, A. S., *The Spanish Inquisition*, London, 1932.

tempted to regard the attitude towards problems of belief embedded in the prayer-book of the Church of England as one that should be unquestioningly accepted, we may reflect that the prayer-book was compiled by people who themselves burned heretics. Obviously there were reasons why such a practice developed, but we have a duty to ask whether they were a justification for it, and, if not, what is a reasonable attitude towards doctrinal differences. We must ask also how much of the attitude towards doctrinal differences which we have inherited from the past needs reconsideration in the light of our answer to the first question.

Can we, for example, continue to be satisfied with the fact that the condemnatory clauses in the Athanasian Creed are still retained in the Church of England prayer-book for public recitation? Let us remind ourselves of how these clauses run in the authorised version of the prayer-book (they were somewhat modified in the revision rejected by Parliament in 1927):

"Whosoever will be saved: before all things it is necessary that he hold the Catholick Faith.

"Which Faith except everyone do keep whole and undefiled: without doubt he shall perish everlastingly.

"And the Catholick Faith is this:

.   .   .   .   .

"He therefore that will be saved; must thus think of the Trinity.

"Furthermore it is necessary to everlasting salvation: that he also believes rightly the Incarnation of our Lord Jesus Christ.

.   .   .   .   .

"This is the Catholick Faith: which except a man believe faithfully, he cannot be saved."

It must, of course, be admitted that some of the force of these phrases results from changes in the use of language since the translation was made. The meaning of the opening clause *Quicumque vult salvus esse* would probably be better conveyed at the present time by "Whoever wishes to be a Christian" or, by Dr. Badcock's rendering, "Whosoever would be in a state of salvation".[1] But even when all misunderstandings due to this cause have been removed, the general meaning that correctness of belief in the propositions of the creed is a necessary condition of salvation remains, and this is the kind of valuation of correctness of belief which was accepted by the translators of the prayer-book and which few Christians now can accept as reflecting the teaching of Christ. This has been said many times before, but the clauses remain for public recitation.

It would, of course, be wrong to suggest that the rulers of the Church of England have been unaware of the uneasiness with which these condemnatory clauses are regarded. A declaration made by the Convocation of the Province of Canterbury in 1873 and reaffirmed in 1879 justified these clauses by pointing out that "Holy Scripture in divers places doth promise life to them that believe, and declare the condemnation of them that believe not".[1] The time has surely come for again reconsidering the matter. It is clear that Holy Scripture does not declare the condemnation of those who do not believe the particular propositions of the Athanasian Creed. One may believe that these propositions are true, or at least as true as can be any

[1] Badcock, F. J., *The History of the Creeds* (2nd edn.), London, 1938.

attempt to express in language the nature of the God-head and of the Incarnation, and yet not consider that belief in them is necessary to salvation. We can believe that they are important without believing that this is the correct way to express their importance.

The use of intemperate language by the early makers of creeds when condemning the heretics with whom they were disagreeing was, of course, still a long way from the practice of burning heretics. It was, however, one step on the road leading Christian believers from the teachings of Christ to the practice of appalling cruelties. If indeed a visitor from Mars had been present at an *auto de Fé* of the Spanish Inquisition or at Norwich Castle when Kett was burned, he might well have asked what such strange scenes had to do with the teachings of Jesus Christ. The linkage is not a direct one, and it is necessary to study something of history and of social psychology to make the derivation intelligible.

The Christian Church was faced very early by the problem of what attitude to adopt towards teachings imported from other religions and towards deviations of doctrine arising from within itself. Such problems are referred to as early as the Epistles of St. Paul. Any religious body can adopt either of two opposed attitudes towards such intrusions or changes of doctrine, either willingly incorporating them or rejecting them. The first is the attitude of tolerance of doctrinal deviations; the second is that of intolerance. A religious body can also, of course, adopt any position between these two extremes of acceptance and rejection. A relatively intolerant attitude does not imply violence towards those responsible for such deviations; it may involve only exclusion from church-membership.

Violent persecution was not found in the early centuries of the Christian Church, although exclusion from membership of persons deviating in teaching from the accepted norm was apparently practised from the beginning. There is, of course, a considerable difference between exclusion for holding wrong opinions and for teaching wrong opinions. There seems no evidence in the New Testament that there was any exclusion from the Church of members merely holding wrong opinions, although it is obvious that if any individual's opinions had been sufficiently different from those held in the early Church he would have been unlikely to want to join that body.

The word "intolerance" has now a bad flavour, but if it is defined merely as a tendency to reject alien and novel teachings, this is not necessarily either bad or good in itself. It may lead to bad things such as persecution, but it may also serve useful ends such as keeping intact a body of teaching that is true and valuable.

The social psychological effects on religious development may be illustrated by the histories of Judaism and Hinduism respectively. The Jewish prophets waged a constant warfare against assimilation of elements of alien religions which were regarded as systems of worship of false gods. Hinduism, on the other hand, has been receptive of gods and rites from various sources with results that Sir Charles Eliot has described by saying: "[Hinduism is] a jungle not a building. It is a living example of a great national paganism such as might have existed in Europe if Christianity had not become the state religion of the Roman Empire, if there had remained an incongruous jumble of old local superstitions, Greek philosophy, and oriental cults such as the worship of Mithra or

Serapis."[1] And, one may add, it is what might have existed in Europe if Christianity, having become the state religion of the Roman Empire, had also been indefinitely tolerant of infiltration from surrounding cults. If its intolerance was justified by the object of keeping a true faith free from the intrusion of religious concepts and practices which would have degraded it, it is also arguable that religious development within Christianity has been impoverished by too stiffly resisting any religious insights that may have been possessed by the saints and sages of other religions, of Hinduism, of Islam, and of Buddhism.

The way of indefinite toleration is also a way in which a religion may develop. It has obvious dangers, but it may be justified by the belief that all concepts of divinity are more or less inadequate symbols of the one inexpressible reality. The Hindu masses may worship at the altars of Vishnu, or Saiva, or Kali, while the Hindu sage holds that all these are symbols of the One for whom no symbol is adequate.

That is a possible way of looking at the diversities of religions, but it is not the way adopted by the early Christian Church or earlier by Judaism. Let us imagine that a Hindu sage had approached Elijah with the plea that it did not matter whether the Jews worshipped Jehovah or Baal since both were symbols of the one inexpressible Godhead. Elijah would have rejected such an idea; to him there was one true God, Jehovah, and the gods of Canaan were false gods to be wholly rejected, their rites prohibited, and their priests destroyed. The massacre of the priests of Baal by the brook Kishon was a typical behaviour-pattern of religious intolerance essentially motivated in the same

[1] Eliot, C., *Hinduism and Buddhism*, London, 1921.

way as such a later persecution as the massacre of the Albigenses. The rational aim in both cases was to preserve a body of religious belief and practice from the intrusion of alien or new elements.

Let us suppose that the prophets of the Old Testament had not succeeded. If Judaism had freely assimilated alien rites and gods, it too would have become a jungle. The seed bed from which Christianity grew would have been unimaginably different.

Intolerance of doctrinal deviations and of intrusions from other religions in Christianity is partly to be explained historically by the fact that it developed from Judaism, which showed a similar intolerance. It is true that the problem in Judaism was primarily that of intrusions and not of deviations from within, but so also was that very largely the problem of the early Christian Church. An attitude of intolerance towards alien intrusions is likely to lead to a similar attitude of intolerance towards deviations developing from within since both have the same object, to keep intact an original body of belief.

Certainly this object was not completely realised. Assimilation of elements from alien faiths did take place in Christianity, and developments of doctrine also took place, but both changes took place against a strong tendency to conservation. Part of the impetus behind the Protestant Reformation was the conviction that there had been too much assimilation and too much development, and the reforming movement was regarded as a return to original Christianity.

But neither the reformers nor their opponents doubted that assimilation and essential change were bad things; they differed only as to how far they had, in fact, taken place.

The essential idea behind resistance to assimilation and change is obviously a defensible one. The resistance may have been too rigid; it certainly used deplorable methods. But it cannot reasonably be denied that the Church has the duty of examining alien teachings and novelties of doctrine, and discarding what is bad in them even if it is also ready to accept what is good in them. The Church has a real function as guardian of the faith which I propose to discuss in a later chapter. The fact that we are now inclined to value tolerance more highly than it was valued in the past is no reason for denying the Church any function as guardian of the faith. Indeed, part of its function as guardian may be to check intolerance, since those introducing novelties of doctrine may be and often are intolerant in their attitudes about them.

If one tries to account for intolerance in its more extreme form of religious persecution, one is inclined to say that it is based on the implicit idea that the unity of a social body depends on all of its members believing the same things. It was as a threat to social unity of Church and of Nation that heretics were persecuted. I do not think this was the implicit idea behind the attempt to obtain doctrinal unity in the early Church Councils. Indeed, a different idea was explicitly stated in the fourth century by the author of the Athanasian Creed. The idea there expressed is that one can only be in a state of salvation if one has correct beliefs on various theological points. This idea may also be wrong, but although it leads to intolerance in the social psychological sense it could not lead to persecution of heretics (of those who merely hold wrong opinions), although it might be a ground for punishing those who taught wrong opinions. It would

D

plainly not be reasonable to execute those who were not in a state of salvation, although it might be reasonable to punish those whose teaching endangered the state of salvation of others.

But this idea can easily grow into the more dangerous one that deviations from the accepted norm of opinion are themselves threats to the social group in which they develop, and by the time that religious persecution was well developed this seems to have been the implicit principle on which the persecutors acted. Yet the question of whether or not the unification of a social group depends on all of its members having the same opinions on important questions is an empirical question in social psychology to be decided by observation of social groups, and it does not appear that this observation gives any ground for believing that this principle is a true one.

Certainly there must be some basis for unity, but this may be supplied by community of interest or of practical aim and not by uniformity of belief. An obvious modern example of this is a scientific society. Members of the British Psychological Society have a common interest in the experimental investigation of problems of human behaviour and thought. But this common interest is accompanied by considerable difference in opinion on the results obtained; indeed, the discussion of this diversity of opinion is part of the common interest. It is not that the difference between one psychological theory and another is regarded as unimportant, or that it is not considered to be important to determine which is the right opinion and which the wrong. But the fact that one individual holds opinions differing from those of the majority on the nature of perception or on the part played by instinct in human behaviour would not be regarded as a ground for seeking his exclusion from the Society. This does not mean that there are no possible grounds for exclusion. An individual not in sympathy with the common aim would normally not be accepted for membership, and a member whose conduct showed him to be pursuing aims in contradiction with those of the Society can be deprived of his membership.

It is possible for a strongly unified religious group also to include wide diversity of opinion on religious questions. Hinduism has already been mentioned as an example of this, but we need not go so far afield; there is also the Church of England. For various historical reasons, a diversity of opinion and practice has developed within the Church of England almost as wide as that between the most different Christian bodies. Yet it remains one community. There is a common opinion that this diversity of opinion is a weakness which must be got rid of by excluding the extremists at both ends and retaining only those who walk in the middle way. The opinion that it is a weakness becomes questionable if we doubt the proposition that the principle of unification of a religious body is necessarily the holding of the same body of beliefs by all its members. One may look at the matter in another way and consider that a unified religious body including divergent opinions held with mutual charity and with mutual intercommunion is the model of a future reunited Christendom. It is clear that if reunion is to depend on the disappearance of differences of opinion it must be postponed to an indefinite future. A considerable step in reunion could be taken now if the basis of unity were regarded as a common aim with mutual tolerance of differences of opinion. The aim as

I imagine it would not be institutional unity but wide intercommunion with mutual tolerance of doctrinal and ritual differences.

There are, of course, psychological reasons for intolerance as well as historical ones. About twenty years ago I made an investigation into the distribution of degrees of certainty with which a group of subjects held various beliefs including religious beliefs.[1] The results were in some degree odd but easily understandable. The oddity was that the degree of certainty shown was not what one would expect if it were determined in a rational manner by the amount of evidence that the subjects had for judging of each opinion's truth or falsity. In that case, one would expect that where opinions for and against a proposition were about equally balanced in numbers, there would be a tendency for both sides to hold their opinions with a low degree of conviction. It was found, on the contrary, that with all opinions, and most particularly with religious opinions, the tendency was either for acceptance or for rejection to be accompanied by a high degree of certainty. It seemed that there was a general tendency for a religious proposition to be either asserted or denied with a high degree of conviction.

This result is, of course, easily understandable if we bear in mind two psychological facts about religious opinions. The first is that either the attitude of belief or disbelief is a stable one, while that of doubt or partial belief is unstable and uncomfortable. Doubts tend, therefore, to be spontaneously suppressed so that the psychologically more agreeable state of a definite opinion one way or the other may be substituted.

[1] Thouless, R. H., "The tendency to certainty in religious beliefs", *British Journal of Psychology*, XXVI, pp. 16-31, Cambridge, 1935.

This suppression has as its psychological effect a high degree of feeling of certainty about the accepted proposition and hostility towards those denying it. This hostility is, no doubt, part of the driving-force behind religious intolerance and persecution. Secondly, religion is a practical activity. If one has chosen an opinion, any thought of the possibility of the truth of its opposite tends to weaken effort and is therefore unserviceable to action. This gives a more rational ground for hostility against those who question one's accepted beliefs. The remedy for the hostility on both grounds would appear to be that we should have a clear awareness of our own uncertainties instead of suppressing them, and also that we should form the habit of acting definitely even when we know that the opinions on which we act are not certainly true. This is a problem of mental hygiene to which I wish to return later.

Chapter Four

THE RELIGIOUS GOAL

THE moral that can be drawn from the sad history of religious persecution is that, at some stage in the development of Christendom, its members went badly wrong in their valuation of correctness of belief. It has already been suggested that this history concerns us, not because we have any duty of finding fault with our ancestors, but because we have the duty of examining critically the attitudes towards correctness of belief which we have inherited from them. It may be that some of the attitudes towards orthodoxy which led to persecution still persist in our own minds, and that these are still obstacles to mutual understanding and charity between Christians who differ in matters of belief. It is generally felt that a more tolerant attitude towards differences of belief is desirable, and we may ask what is a reasonable attitude towards problems of religious belief that would justify such wider tolerance.

If tolerance is to be defended it must be on rational grounds; we cannot be satisfied with a tolerance that is achieved at the price of undervaluing truth or of refusing to think clearly. We cannot, for example, be content to say that it does not matter what we believe. We have an intellectual duty to do our best to attain right opinions in religion even if this may mean that other people disagree with us. This duty is at least as binding as that of seeing that our opinions are right in matters belonging to the realm of science. It is not merely a duty on the intellectual plane since both our social and our devotional life depend to a considerable extent on what religious propositions we accept and what we reject. Athanasius and Arius differed in their opinions of the nature of Christ, but they would have been in complete agreement on the proposition that it mattered whether one thought of Christ as God or as a creation by God. They would both have recognised the intellectual duty of getting one's opinions as right as possible on such a question, and they would also have recognised that one's devotional attitudes would be influenced by which side one embraced in this controversy.

Nor can we safely achieve tolerance by the conviction that all beliefs are the same or are, at worst, different aspects of the same truth. This may sometimes be the case, but to suggest that it is always or necessarily the case is to abandon clear thinking. It is plain that some of the religious propositions about which men differ can be stated sufficiently clearly for it to be possible to say that both cannot be right. It may certainly be very difficult to find coercive reasons for concluding which (if either) is right, but if one man says that Jesus Christ was born of a virgin and another says that he was the son of Joseph, they mean different things. If either is right, the other must be wrong. So also do they mean different things when one man says that the Eucharist is a sacrifice and another says that it is a memorial service, or if one says that Jesus Christ was the only-begotten Son of God while another says that he was one of a large number of incarnations of God. There are real differences in religious opinions, and a reasonably grounded tolerance does not require that we should say that those who differ from us can never be wrong. It does require that we should recognise that they have a right to be wrong when making judgments on questions which cannot be coercively settled, and that we also may be sometimes wrong, and also that whether we or they are wrong, the holding of a mistaken opinion does not entail that the holder of it may not be more truly a servant of God than one who has the good fortune to hold a right opinion.

If this be admitted, it remains true that something was wrong in the attitude towards orthodoxy which led to persecution. I suggest that the basic error may be best described as that of regarding correctness of belief as the goal of the Christian religion. Such an implicit belief is still to be found; it may be expressed in some such form as the statement that the traditional creeds or other formulations of Christian doctrine *are* the Christian faith. I suggest that this idea must be uncompromisingly rejected. It may have been what Torquemada thought, but I do not think it would have been accepted by St. Athanasius or St. Augustine. The early Church Councils who were engaged in formulating the creeds would, I think, have considered themselves to be safeguarding the Christian faith. But the faith they were safeguarding was something other than the structure they were erecting to safeguard it.

The doctrinal system of a religion may be regarded as analogous to a map. A man who is performing a journey may have a map which serves the purpose of guiding him to his goal and which does so by giving him information about the country through which he must travel. Trust in the map may be a means for reaching his goal, but trust in the map is not itself the goal. The mere affirmation by the traveller that the map is correct in all its parts will not in itself carry him to his journey's end.

The goal itself is the Christian way of living. Many attempts have been made to find a brief phrase which would express the essence of this goal, as, for example, Harnack's "The Fatherhood of God and the Brotherhood of Man",[1] or the common appeal of the evangelistic preacher, "All you have to do is to accept Jesus Christ as your personal saviour". The danger of all such attempts is that they tend to oversimplify a complicated system of demands by picking out one part of the Gospel message while overlooking other parts.

We have, however, one shortened statement of the Christian goal which has the authority of Jesus Christ himself: "Thou shalt love the Lord thy God with all thy heart, and with all thy soul, and with all thy strength, and with all thy mind; and thy neighbour as thyself" [Luke x, 27, A.V.]. There is no oversimplification here. It is a programme so vast that we must all recognise our failure to attain it, so complex that all the references to Christian duties in the Gospels and other sacred writings can be regarded as amplifications of it.

It is a great contribution of Kierkegaard to religious thought that he constantly reminds us of this goal of the Christian life,[2] and invites us to measure the value of such religious accessories as creeds, ceremonies, and rules of behaviour, by considering how far they lead us towards this goal and how far we have allowed them instead to become substitute goals. He quoted with approval a remark attributed to Pascal, that Christendom is a society of people who with the help of certain

---

[1] Harnack, A. von., *What is Christianity?* (Eng. trans.), London, 1901.
[2] Kierkegaard, S., *Works of Love*, 1847 (Eng. trans., Princeton, N.J., 1946).

sacraments evade the duty of loving God.[1] One might vary this remark by putting in other substitute goals. Religious dogmas may be for some people a system of beliefs whose acceptance is felt to exempt them from the duty of loving God and their neighbours. For others it may be a system of behaviour prohibitions (of drinking, of profane swearing, or of working or amusing themselves on Sundays). All these elements, religious ceremonies, religious beliefs, and the acceptance of behaviour prohibitions, may be means towards the attainment of the religious goal; all are dangerous when they become substitute goals.

Kierkegaard realised that the Christian goal as expressed by Christ was in general unattainable even to the most devout, so he preferred to speak of himself and others not as being Christians but as becoming Christians, that is, not as having attained the Christian goal but as being on the path towards it. While this succeeds in making a forcible presentation of his point of view, it is at the cost of doing some violence to the ordinary use of language. It is a purely verbal question whether a Christian shall be defined as one who is on the way to the Christian goal or as one who has attained it. Kierkegaard was adopting the second definition, but the first is the more common use of the word 'Christian'. If we adopt the ordinary usage of the word 'Christian', Kierkegaard's point can still be made by saying that the Christian is on his way to the Christian goal and has not arrived there. That is no doubt important, but it may be said without doing violence to the customary use of language.

The substitute goal with which we are here con-

[1] Kierkegaard, S., *Journal*, 1854, quoted from R. Jolivet, *Introduction to Kierkegaard* (Eng. trans.), London, 1950.

cerned is that of adherence to orthodox doctrine; the psychological roots of the kind of intolerance that led to religious persecution may be regarded as the adoption of correctness of doctrine as a substitute goal in place of that of loving God and one's neighbour. Other roots of intolerance are clearly possible; ceremonial might be adopted as a substitute goal and those might be persecuted who showed deviations in ritual practice, or behaviour prohibitions might become a substitute goal leading to persecution of those who carried out prohibited lines of behaviour. Both of these types of persecution have, in fact, occurred, but persecution of unorthodox belief or teaching has been of overwhelmingly greater volume and it may therefore be considered as the main problem of religious intolerance.

From the point of view suggested by the analogy between the functions of a doctrinal system and those of a map, this acceptance of orthodoxy as a substitute goal of the religious journey may be regarded as analogous to the case of a man who forgets that his map is a means of getting somewhere and supposes that belief in the correctness of the map is an end in itself.

This analogy has also other implications which may be worth exploring. The possession of a good map may be a useful means of reaching the journey's end, but it is not a sufficient means to that end and it may not be a necessary means. We may have a good map and fail to reach the intended end of our journey, while others with less good maps may succeed better. If so, their achievement of the goal is more important than the imperfections of their map. Yet this consideration does not make unimportant the question of which map is the most correct. It is right that we should try to make as good as possible both our own maps and those we provide other people, since a good map is better than a bad one as a means of reaching the goal, even though men may reach the goal with an imperfect map.

However strongly we may believe that our own doctrinal system is the best available, we must recognise that there are members of other Christian bodies who hold a somewhat different system of beliefs whose sanctity shows that they are nearer to the Christian goal than we are ourselves. In all Christian sects it seems to be the case that those who are nearer to God are more like each other than they are to those of their own denomination who belong more to the World. When those who are saints talk of the more central part of their religious life, they seem generally to talk in so much the same way that it is difficult to tell to what religious denomination they belong, although they may talk very differently on peripheral religious matters. If this is the case, it is a fact that must be borne in mind in evaluating correctness of belief, although it need not entail that correctness of belief is of no importance.

It is perhaps more disturbing to have forced on our attention the fact that there appear to be saints in other religions than Christianity, and that when a religious mystic talks of God, it may be impossible to know whether the one talking is a Roman Catholic, a Quaker, a Moslem, a Hindu, or of the Jewish faith. Let us, for example, consider some typical mystical utterances:

(1) "When I love God with my will, I transform myself into Him, for this is the power or virtue of love, that it maketh thee to be like unto that which thou lovest."

(2) "When the love of God arises in thy heart, without doubt God also feels love for thee."

(3) "One should have such burning faith in God that one can say: 'What? I have repeated the name of God, and can sin still cling to me? How can I be a sinner any more?'"

(4) "Whatever is, is in God, and nothing can exist or be conceived without God."

These are utterances belonging to the central core of religion and there is little in their character that would enable a reader to identify the first as written by a Christian (St. Bernard[1]), the second by a Moslem (Jalalu 'd Din[1]), the third by a Hindu (Sri Ramakrishna[2]), and the fourth by a Jew (Spinoza[3]).

Even if we accept the view that those holding widely different dogmatic systems may attain the same goal of love of God and of their fellow-men, this does not entail many of the consequences that are sometimes drawn from it. For example, it does not entail: (1) that doctrinal systems serve no function in religion and that they should be discarded in favour of a "religion without dogma"; (2) that all doctrinal systems of different Christian bodies or of different religions are equally true; or (3) that the rational course is to discard all that is peculiar to one's own religious system and to retain only what is common to all religions, a course that is sometimes described as passing from a religion to Religion or as that of embracing the perennial philosophy common to all religions.[4]

None of these apparent implications seems particularly plausible if we regard the function of a system of

[1] Underhill, Evelyn, *Mysticism*, London, 1911.
[2] Ghanananda, *Sri Ramakrishna*, Mylapore, Madras, 1946.
[3] Spinoza, *Ethics* (Eng. trans. by A. Boyle), London, 1910.
[4] Huxley, A., *The Perennial Philosophy*, London, 1946.

religious doctrine as analogous to that of a map.
Because more than one sort of map may enable a man
to reach the point towards which he is journeying, it
cannot be safely concluded that he would have got
there equally well without any map at all. Particular
systems of religious doctrine may be in part erroneous;
where they differ it is indeed plain that some at least
must be partly erroneous. Awareness of the possibility
of error even in our own beliefs may be a good thing,
promoting a tolerance of the apparent errors of others,
but it is not reasonable to be so afraid of the risk of
error as to abandon altogether factual guidance in the
religious field.

Moreover, the fact that a man may get to his goal
with an imperfect map does not imply that one map
may not be better and more correct than another. The
sensible course in travelling is to use the best map
available. In religious thinking also, we have the duty
to assure ourselves so far as we can that the system of
doctrine we assent to is as true as it can be. Here too
we may gain in tolerance and understanding of those
who differ from us if we reflect that although the
question of relative truth of different systems of religious doctrines is a real one, it is also one about which
it is difficult for us to make an entirely rational judgment, and that our conviction that our own beliefs are
nearer to the truth than those we reject may be largely
the product of our own habits of thought resulting from
the traditions in which we have been brought up.

Still less does the fact that men may reach the goal
by different maps imply that we should use a map
which contains only what is common to all maps. A
particular map may contain errors and yet be a better
guide than a relatively featureless general map. It is

better that men should adopt a particular system of religious beliefs while remaining aware of the existence of other systems and of the true saintliness of some of the followers of those other systems. Mutual tolerance rather than confusion of beliefs is the desirable fruit of such awareness. If many systems of religious beliefs may indicate the road to God, some may be better guides than others; one may be the right guide for ourselves.

It may be objected that tolerance based on such a view would destroy the motivation for missionary effort. I think it changes rather than destroys it. One can fully accept the view that all religions are roads to God and yet believe that Christianity is the best road, better than those other systems we call the "higher religions" and incomparably better than primitive paganism. The matter has been well expressed by Simone Weil: "All religions pronounce the name of God in their particular language. As a rule it is better for a man to name God in his native tongue rather than in one that is foreign to him. . . . A change of religion is for the soul like a change of language for a writer. All religions it is true are not equally suitable for the recitation of the name of the Lord. Some without any doubt are very imperfect mediums."[1]

[1] Weil, S., *Waiting on God* (Eng. trans.), London, 1951.

Chapter Five

RELIGIOUS LANGUAGE

A FURTHER resemblance between a religious doctrinal system and a map lies in the fact that a map uses a system of conventional signs—two curved lines for a bridge, a cross for a church, and so on—the understanding of which is necessary for the proper use of the map. One would gravely misunderstand the map if the conventional nature of these signs were not recognised and if one supposed that the object represented looked like the conventional sign on the map, i.e. if one supposed that the map were a picture. One would also be making a mistake if one regarded the map as a bad map because the objects indicated did not look like their conventional signs. The system of conventional signs is a kind of language which is used by the map maker and must be understood by the map user; the language of visual representation might also have been used (as in a photograph taken from the air), but for many purposes this would be less convenient.

It is easy to recognise that in a large number of religious statements a somewhat parallel situation arises. We have such statements as: "The Lord is my Shepherd", "There's a home for little children, above the bright blue sky", or "Unto you that fear my name shall the Sun of righteousness arise with healing in his wings [Malachi iv, 2]". One would obviously misunderstand such passages if one supposed that they were literal descriptive statements.

Similar use of language is found sometimes in non-religious statements. We may, for example, say that the exchequer axe has come down on school building when what we mean could be expressed literally by saying that an instruction has been sent to local education authorities to reduce their expenditure on building schools. There is, however, in religious statements the special reason for the prevalence of this language usage that our ordinary language has been evolved as an instrument for purposes connected with the world of physical objects and of other human personalities (for describing them, for expressing attitudes towards them, for influencing conduct with respect to them, and so on), and is not adequate for the purpose of talking about the objects of religion which are not physical objects or human personalities.

Language can nevertheless be used for conveying religious ideas when it cannot literally describe religious objects; more can be shown in religion by the use of language than can be said. One of the ways in which language can be used to convey religious ideas is by the use of such expressions as "The Lord is my shepherd".

This use of language is often called that of 'religious symbolism'. This term has traditional justification, it was used in the fifth century by "Dionysius the Areopagite".[1] Nevertheless, it has become an awkward term for current use since the word "symbolism" has now generally a wider use to cover the use of any word or mark on paper to stand for an object, quality, relation, etc. Thus we call the word 'dog' a symbol of the class of dogs and the word 'two' or the figure '2' symbols of the class of $1+1$ objects. It seems better, therefore, to call such language usage as that embodied

[1] Dionysius the Areopagite, *On the Heavenly Hierarchy* (Eng. trans. by John Parker), London, 1899.

E

in "The Lord is my shepherd" the metaphorical use of language rather than the symbolic use of language. Religious metaphors will then be spoken of as one sub-class of the class of religious symbols, while other religious symbols are ritual actions and the technical terms of a system of theology.

The common use of metaphorical expressions in religion may be a real difficulty to the non-religious person who feels drawn towards religion. He may feel that the acceptance of religion would commit him to the acceptance of propositions which no sensible person can believe. Indeed, many of the statements of religious thought would be absurd if they were understood as literal statements. They are not intended to be so understood. In order to understand any language, it is necessary to know its symbols and the method of their use. One who would understand religious thought must learn the symbols of metaphorical language and their customary usage. The failure to understand them which results from mistaking them for the more usual literal use of language leads to a misinterpretation of religious thought which makes nonsense of a great part of it.

The suggestion that much religious thought is conveyed by metaphor is often regarded as a modern sophistication by which the believer tries to justify himself in accepting the traditional statements of religion after he has emancipated himself from the ideas which they originally embodied. There seems, however, to be no reason for supposing that he is doing otherwise than understanding them as they were meant to be understood by those who wrote them.

H. G. Wells wrote, for example, "The personal appearance of the Christian God is described in The Revelation, and however much that description may be explained away by commentators as symbolical, it is certainly taken by most straightforward believers as a statement of concrete reality."[1] The main point of interest in this passage is, I think, its suggestion that those who regard such a description as "symbolical" are not being "straightforward". This would be a reasonable reproach if such religious statements had been regarded in the past as literal description and the understanding of them as metaphor were a modern subterfuge to make it possible to accept the verbal form of these statements while disbelieving their original content. That this is the case could not be supposed by anyone familiar with the writings of Aquinas or Dionysius or who had read the first Article of Religion in the English prayer-book: "There is but one living and true God, everlasting, without body, parts, or passions."

It is, however, not only those unfamiliar with traditional religious thought who suggest that the understanding of the difference between the metaphorical and the literal use of language is a recent achievement of human thought. We also find in George Tyrrell's *Christianity at the Cross Roads*: "For Jesus, what we call His apocalyptic 'imagery' was no mere imagery but literal fact. But for us it can be so no longer. We can no longer believe in the little local Heaven above the flat earth, from which Jesus is to appear in the clouds: nor in all the details of the vision governed by this conception." And later: "To pretend that Jesus regarded His apocalyptic portrayal of the transcendent as symbolic [i.e. metaphorical] is to pretend that his mind belonged to the nineteenth century."[2]

[1] Wells, H. G., *God the Invisible King*, London, 1917.
[2] Tyrrell, G., *Christianity at the Cross Roads*, London, 1910.

This seems to me to be a complete misunderstanding of the situation; realisation of the difference between the metaphorical and the literal uses of language was not a discovery of the nineteenth century. We need not follow Tyrrell in making the question more difficult by mixing it up with the problem of the limitations of the human knowledge of Jesus, but would his statement be true of the contemporaries of Jesus? It seems rather more likely that to them metaphor was so much a natural and familiar method of expression that the literal interpretation of metaphorical speech would have been unlikely.

One cannot be sure of this since it is not until confusion between metaphorical and literal expression has taken place that the difference between them will be discussed. It was certainly discussed a long time before Tyrrell's day. In the fourteenth century, the anonymous author of *The Cloud of Unknowing* warned his readers not to mistake metaphorical language about spiritual things for literal language about material things. "Be wary", he said, "that thou conceive not bodily that which is meant ghostly, although it be spoken in bodily words, as be these, up or down, in or out, behind or before."[1] Particularly, he warned his readers against the error of supposing that there was a localised heaven: "For heaven ghostly is as nigh down as up, and up as down, behind as before, before as behind, on one side as other." Nearly a thousand years earlier than this, the fifth-century writer who called himself "Dionysius the Areopagite" discussed the use of metaphor in religious language and certainly had no tendency to treat as literal the statements of Scripture

[1] Anonymous, *The Cloud of Unknowing* (edited by Evelyn Underhill), London, 1950.

which the modern reader would regard as metaphorical. He wrote: "In order that we also may not, like the vulgar, irreverently think that the heavenly and Godlike minds are certain many-footed and many-faced creatures . . . and should imagine that there are certain wheels of fire above the heaven, or material thrones upon which the Godhead may recline . . . and whatever else was transmitted by the Oracles [i.e. by the Scriptures] to us under multifarious symbols of sacred imagery."[1]

It is not, of course, to be denied that there has been much literalism amongst religious persons, as apparently there was in the fifth century amongst those whom Dionysius called "the vulgar". No doubt H. G. Wells did have presented to him the Apocalyptic picture of God on his Throne as literal description and so came to regard this literalism as standard Christian belief. No doubt also Father Tyrrell had met people who believed in a local heaven. Nevertheless, such literalism did not belong to the orthodox Catholic tradition; Dionysius belonged to that tradition and his orthodoxy was unquestioned by St. Thomas Aquinas.

I suggest that the confusion between metaphor and literal statement is not a characteristic of early Christian thought, but rather of modern times. The language of metaphor is no longer natural to us. The development of the exact sciences has had as a secondary consequence a tendency for education to be in the direction of using language in a way that avoids ambiguity, whereas multiplicity of reference is a characteristic of the metaphorical use of language. It is not only our religious thinking that is affected by our increased

[1] Dionysius the Areopagite, *On the Heavenly Hierarchy* (Eng. trans. by John Parker), London, 1899.

literalism. The modern man is likely to find T. S. Eliot's *The Waste Land* as unintelligible as the Apocalypse, and for much the same reason: because it uses language in a way he is not accustomed to. He is inclined, therefore, not to accept metaphorical language as something that can be understood by acquiring the technique of its use, but as something that must either be understood as itself the language of literal description (which makes its statements generally absurd) or must be made intelligible by translation from metaphor into the literal language.

We can, to some extent, overcome the difficulties of understanding metaphorical poetry by translating it into the literal language, although this translation results in impoverishment since it abandons the multiplicity of reference which is characteristic of the use of metaphor. The translation of religious metaphor, however, meets with the further difficulty that ordinary language, having been evolved as an instrument for the practical ends of dealing with a world of material objects, is not an adequate instrument for describing realities of another order. When we try to translate religious metaphor into the language of literalism we are liable to find either that we have made a statement so unclear as to be useless for communication or that we have substituted a new metaphor for an old one.

An example of an attempted translation from religious metaphor to literalism may be found in a translation of the Apostles' Creed made by the Abbé Hébert, which began: "I believe in the objective value of the idea of God, of an absolute ideal, perfect, distinct, inseparable from the world which it draws and leads towards the Better, the principle of all physical and moral appearances. . . ."[1] Much is lost in intelligibility, and there is no real escape from metaphor; 'distinct' and 'inseparable' are both spatial metaphors.

I would suggest that all attempts to get rid of metaphor from religious statements (or to "demythologise" them) are mistaken. We can acquire the technique of the metaphorical use of language as we can acquire other skills. If we want to understand religious thought, either to affirm it or to deny it, it is necessary that we should acquire this technique. Then we can agree to talk of God as if he were a person, of Heaven as if it were a place, of ascending to Heaven as if it were a direction, all with the implicit proviso: "This must not be understood literally."

The use of metaphor to refer to spiritual realities does not, of course, imply that these are regarded as any less real than the physical objects referred to in the literal use of language. In an unpublished book, I recently read the statement: "When God is spoken of as the Sun of Righteousness this is no mere metaphor." It is, of course, a metaphor, but one must question the implication of the word 'mere'. What the writer had in mind was, I think, that what was meant by "Sun of Righteousness" was something as real as what is referred to when one talks of the sun in the sky. But when it is said that the phrase is a metaphor, it is not implied that what is spoken of is in some way unreal; the word 'metaphor' describes the use of language, not some property of the thing spoken about.

One cannot properly ask of a metaphorical statement whether it is true or false, for other metaphors might also be used to indicate the same thing. One

[1] de la Bedoyère, M., *The Life of Baron von Hügel*, 1950.

can properly ask whether or to what extent the metaphor is adequate. The test of adequacy is whether it leads to understanding of and appropriate behaviour with respect to the thing referred to. No religious metaphor can be wholly adequate since it cannot in itself lead to full understanding of what it is intended to indicate. Some metaphors may be very inadequate; some may be inadequate guides to spiritual reality when taken by themselves and not in relation to other metaphors dealing with the same subject-matter.

There is a well-known metaphorical portrayal of God as a monarch in the Revelation of St. John the Divine: "He that sat [on the throne] was to look upon like a jasper and a sardine stone: and there was a rainbow round about the throne, in sight like unto an emerald . . . and out of the throne proceeded lightnings and thunderings and voices" (Rev. iv, 3, 5). That this is a metaphorical description is at once apparent. It is a use of words to indicate what cannot be said and to indicate also the fact of the impossibility of literal description.

We may also speak of God as our heavenly father. That too is a metaphor and one that has the authority of our Lord Jesus Christ. The second is a metaphor that is likely to seem more appropriate to a modern man since he has lost much of the feeling that St. John would have had for monarchs. Yet St. John's metaphor has this advantage, that we cannot overlook the fact that it is a metaphor. It is easier to forget that the picture of the heavenly father is also a metaphor, and not a literal statement or a full picture of the relation of God to ourselves. While Jesus Christ used that metaphor in his parables, he also used others which pictured God as a landowner on whose land we have the duty of work-ing, as a master whose servants we are, as a shepherd, as a judge, and so on. All contribute to the conception of God presented in the Gospels.

A very inadequate conception of God may result from selecting one of these symbols to the neglect of all the others. The decay of religious faith may result from a concept of God which is not much more than that of a kindly old gentleman in the sky whose prime con-cern is with our comfort. Doubts may arise when it is found that our earthly comfort is less complete than one would expect from so kindly and powerful a guardian.

Individual records of the development of religious unbelief show such cases as the following. "I was taught that God answers prayer. I prayed for fine weather at our school picnic and it rained. After that my faith in God went away." The teachers of that child have a grave responsibility for having given it a concept of God so little capable of lasting through the stresses of life. It might have happened that the weather was fine at the picnic, and the inadequate concept would have been for the moment reinforced, but it would have remained dangerously unstable. It may not be possible to give a young child a concept of God which is the same as that of an adult faith; it is neces-sary, however, that his religious education should give him a concept of God on which his adult faith can be built.

The concept of God as a mere benevolent universal provider is a degenerate religious symbol neither in accordance with Christian tradition nor adequate to enable man to master his own internal problems and to have a religious understanding of those outside

himself. It is, I think, even a degeneration of the metaphor of the father. The earthly father is to a child not
merely a kindly protector; he is also an object of
respect, one whose actions towards the child may be
frustrating rather than comforting, and one also who
has a life of his own with ends remote from the interests
of the child. At least so much must have entered into
the idea of the Father to those who heard our Lord's
parables where this metaphor was used, and much more
into the total complex of metaphorical representation
of God as father, landowner, master, shepherd, and
judge.

These other elements are neglected if the concept of
God is derived too exclusively from the metaphor of
the father. They include wonder, majesty, and terror.
These also are found in the concept of God as presented in the Scriptures, in the Catholic tradition, and
in the intuitions of the mystics. Certainly it is essential
to the Christian tradition that behind the majesty and
wonder and terror there is Divine love. The most
adequate symbolic representation of God is that which
includes both of these sets of elements, as when the
Lady Julian writes that she "was astonied for wonder
and marvel that I had, that He that is so reverend and
dreadful will be so homely with a sinful creature living
in wretched flesh".[1]

The symbol of the Divine Father is not, however,
the only metaphor which, taken in isolation, may
produce an immature and inadequate concept of God.
The convenience of using the idea of God as a means
of producing conformity to adult standards of behaviour
amongst the young may lead to an equal overemphasis

[1] Lady Julian, *Revelations of Divine Love* (edited by Grace Warrack),
London, 1901.

on the metaphor of the Divine judge. I find in Jahoda's investigation of sources of unbelief the following starting-point for decline of religious faith: "I recollect once being upset by a friend swearing and then being surprised that he was not struck down dead."[1] A loss of belief in this case resulted from the observation of a failure of direct Divine action to punish sin, but the deeper cause of the loss of faith apparently lies in the provision by adult teaching of a gravely inadequate conception of God.

Recognition of the prevalence of metaphor in religious language does not imply that all religious language is metaphorical. For example, we find also religious imperatives, religious historical statements, and propositions in the technical language of theology.

Religious imperatives are those which prescribe patterns of behaviour: "Love one another", "Thou shalt not steal", or "Resist not evil". These are using language in its ordinary every-day use since they are not indicating the unsayable, but, on the contrary, carrying out one of the primary functions of language, that is, trying to influence behaviour. Nevertheless, in a social setting in which metaphorical expression was natural and common, imperatives also may be conveyed in metaphorical form: "Let your light so shine before men that they may see your good works", "Whosoever shall smite thee on thy right cheek, turn to him the other also".

Examples of historical statements are those to be found in the Apostles' Creed: "born of the Virgin Mary, suffered under Pontius Pilate, was crucified, dead, and buried". Much of the sacred writings in the

<hr>

[1] Jahoda, G., *The Genesis of non-Belief* (unpublished).

Christian Scriptures, as in those of Buddhism, are ostensibly history, and are, no doubt, intended to be understood as records of past events. Their religious meaning may indeed be related to metaphor in the sense that they too are intended to indicate spiritual realities which cannot be said.

A tradition of treating religious history as both a record of past events and also a metaphorical statement of spiritual facts is an ancient one and belongs to the orthodox tradition. On the other hand, the treatment of such history as solely metaphor has been very generally condemned as erroneous, as, for example, the idea that the crucifixion of Jesus Christ was not a historical event but a metaphor of a spiritual event which must happen in every soul on its way to the religious goal.

It is also possible, however, that an account which has the verbal form of a recital of historical events is, in fact, fiction and was intended by its writer to be read as fiction. At one time a view of the inerrancy of Scripture was adopted which made men unwilling to believe that any of the sacred books were written as fiction and were intended to be read as such, but it would be now commonly agreed that some at least were, for example, the Book of Tobit in the Apocrypha, the Book of Job in the Old Testament, and the story of Adam and Eve in the early chapters of the Book of Genesis. If this view is accepted, the religious value of these books must be regarded as dependent on their adequacy as metaphorical expressions of spiritual truths.

There is also a way of attempting to transcend the limitations of ordinary language without resort to metaphor. This is by the creation of a technical language to express religious ideas whose terms will stand for spiritual objects, qualities, and relations. Such creation of a technical language when ordinary language proves inadequate is a device which is used in the sciences. In religious thinking it is the creation of a theology.

A scientific proposition is a way of expressing a number of interrelated experimental or observational facts. It is a more economical way of referring to the facts than by their enumeration, but it does not add anything new to them. A theological proposition is an economical way of referring to a group of what are regarded as spiritual facts by the religious man. The original data may be statements in the Scriptures or statements of inner experiences by mystical individuals. Either of these may be originally expressed metaphorically. The theological proposition adds nothing to the original data; it merely systematises them.

Let us, for example, consider a typical credal statement. The doctrine of the Trinity is thus stated in the Athanasian Creed: "The Catholic Faith is this: That we worship one God in Trinity and Trinity in Unity; Neither confounding the Persons: nor dividing the Substance." The original data from Scripture and religious experience are the belief that God is one and that Jesus Christ was God and the Holy Spirit was God. The first clause says that God must be thought of as One and also as Three.

The second clause adds nothing to this except a linguistic point. In effect, it defines the words 'person' and 'substance' as they are to be used here. These meanings are not those of ordinary speech; this is an example of redefining a term to give it a technical theological meaning. Other words could have been

used or a non-verbal symbol could have been substituted. In other words, this part of the creed embodies
a linguistic convention. What is said could have been
said in other ways, and one formulation is not
necessarily preferable to another provided it expresses the essential point that God is One and God
is Three.

Thus the creation of a technical theological vocabulary does not really get over the difficulty that language
is an inadequate instrument for saying the central
things about spiritual realities. Those who created the
creeds were aware of this difficulty; they needed verbal
formulae that excluded erroneous ways of thinking and
talking about religious objects, not verbal formulae
that were adequate to express the realities themselves.
Thus Hilary of Poitiers said: "The errors of heretics
and blasphemers force us to deal with unlawful
matters, to scale perilous heights, to speak unutterable
words, to trespass on forbidden ground. Faith ought in
silence to fulfil the commandments, worshipping the
Father, reverencing with Him the Son, abounding in
the Holy Spirit, but we must strain the poor resources
of our language to express thoughts too great for words.
The error of others compels us to err in daring to
embody in human terms truths which ought to be
hidden in the silent veneration of the heart."[1] This
expresses the situation very clearly. Language is an
inadequate instrument for saying things about the
nature of God, and verbal attempts to express the
inexpressible must lead to error (i.e. to inadequacy
of statement), however successful they may be in

[1] Hilary of Poitiers, *De Trinitate* (about 350), quoted from "The
Trinity; meaning or mystery", Cross, L. B., *The Modern Churchman*, XL,
pp. 275-87, Oxford, 1950.

their primary object of excluding other more serious errors.

The impression that I gain from reading modern anti-dogmatic literature is that its writers are often repelled by the apparent claim of dogmas and creeds to express the inexpressible. That this appearance is illusory is strongly suggested by such a passage as that just quoted. It is indeed only one expression of a tendency which ran side by side with the construction of verbal formulations of religious dogmas. It may be called the tendency of "religious agnosticism" from the term *agnosia* used by its most notable exponent, "Dionysius the Areopagite". It is expressed in the following passage: "We must not then dare to speak, or indeed to form any conception, of the hidden super-essential Godhead, except those things that are revealed to us from the Holy Scriptures. For a super-essential understanding of It is proper to Unknowing [agnosia], which lieth in the Super-Essence Thereof surpassing Discourse, Intuition and Being."[1] And in the final passage of *The Mystical Theology*: "Nor can any affirmation or negation apply to it. . . . It transcends all affirmation by being the perfect and unique Cause of all things, and transcends all negation by the pre-eminence of Its simple and absolute nature—free from every limitation and beyond them all."[2]

Perhaps a better known exponent of this point of view is the anonymous author of *The Cloud of Unknowing*, who wrote that to the question, "How shall I think on Himself and what is He?" he could only answer "I wot not", and went on to say "of God Himself can no man

[1] Dionysius the Areopagite, *The Divine Names* (Eng. trans. by C. E. Rolt), London, 1920.
[2] Dionysius the Areopagite, *The Mystical Theology* (Eng. trans. by C. E. Rolt), London, 1920.

think. . . . By love may he be gotten and holden; but by thought never."[1]

This agnostic tendency is not one opposed to the tendency to verbal clarification, but rather one that conditioned it and made it something other than is supposed both by modern dogmatists and by modern anti-dogmatists. St. Thomas Aquinas, the greatest of the verbal clarifiers, showed the strong influence of Dionysius, as when he spoke of the principal method to be followed in treating of the Divine essence as that of *remotion* (the *negative way* of Dionysius): "For the divine essence by its immensity surpasses every form to which our intellect reaches; and thus we cannot apprehend it by knowing what it is. But we have some knowledge thereof by knowing *what it is not*; and we shall approach all the nearer to the knowledge thereof according as we shall be enabled to remove by our intellect a greater number of things therefrom."[2]

I think it may be that the traditional system of belief is made more difficult of acceptance to the honest enquirer because this element of agnosticism in the thought of the systematisers and creed makers has been so much lost sight of during the last few centuries. Such an enquirer may find it difficult to believe that anything can be known as clearly about Divine things as they seem to be stated in the creeds, not realising that the creed makers did not suppose themselves to be solving mysteries but affirming the existence of irresolvable mysteries. He may be repelled by the homely metaphors of the Divine nature used by Christians, not understanding that these are to be understood as ways

[1] Anonymous, *The Cloud of Unknowing* (edited by Evelyn Underhill), London, 1950.

[2] Aquinas, Thomas, *Summa contra Gentiles* (Eng. trans. by D'Arcy M.C., in *Thomas Aquinas: selected writings*), London, 1939.

of showing something that it is beyond the power of words to say. It does not indeed matter how simple or how homely are the symbols of religion so long as it is not forgotten that behind these symbols lies a reality which no words can express and no thought can reach.

F

Chapter Six

RELIGIOUS AUTHORITY

THE modern reaction against the old rigidity of demands as to what the Christian might be allowed to believe has led many people to the idea that the Church has no function as guardian of the faith. Many devout Christians are disposed to echo the words of Berdyaev when he says: "As a free thinker I cannot submit to or admit any tutelage or censorship of my thought; but my thought is deeply rooted in an initial act of faith."[1] We may well agree that the function of the Church is not that of tutelage or censorship of the beliefs of its members, but it does not follow that it has no function in relation to Christian belief or that (as is sometimes now said) the whole conception of heresy is out of date. The matter is not really so simple. Persecutions for heresy are happily out of date, and few would wish to see them revived or would wish to see retained in Christian thinking those attitudes of mind that led to them. But no Church can escape responsibility for controlling what is taught to its members.

Let us suppose that a Church was as liberal as possible and was based on the fundamental principle that all of its members could believe exactly what seemed right to themselves without any restrictions. It would not have escaped the problem of heresy. This would arise as soon as one of its accredited ministers offended against this fundamental principle by teaching his

[1] Berdyaev, N., *Dream and Reality* (Eng. trans.), London, 1950.

congregation that they must believe in some particular dogma and that if they did not they were not true Christians. He might teach his congregation that it was necessary to being in a state of salvation that they should believe in the verbal inspirations of the Scriptures, or in the doctrine of justification by faith, or in the bodily assumption of the Blessed Virgin Mary. The liberal Church we have imagined would be under the necessity to condemn such teaching or else to renounce its fundamental principle. This is not a fantastic supposition. It has always been one of the problems of heresy that the Church has to take action against such of its commissioned ministers as teach requirements more rigorous than those imposed by the Church, whether the rigorism be of behaviour or of doctrine.

Simone Weil may be taken as an example of a modern devout Christian believer who was strongly repelled by the exclusivism and intolerance she found in the Church. She gave as one of her reasons for not being baptised in the Roman Catholic Church her revulsion against the words "Let him be anathema". She spoke of " . . . an insurmountable obstacle to the incarnation of Christianity. It is the use of the two little words *anathema sit*. . . . It is that also which prevents me from crossing the threshold of the Church."[1]

This protest finds an echo in the hearts of most of us. Whether or not the phrase is ever justifiable, it seems often to have been used in a way difficult to defend. It does, however, occur very early in Christian literature. It is used by St. Paul in the Epistle to the Galatians (I, 9). "If any man preach any other gospel to you than that ye have received, let him be accursed." One may,

[1] Weil, S., *Waiting on God* (Eng. trans.), London, 1951.

however, feel less inclined to regard this as evidence of intolerance in St. Paul when one realises that the other gospel he referred to was an over-rigorous one, not a liberating one. The question at issue was whether the keeping of the Mosaic Law was a necessity for a gentile in order that he should be a Christian. Plainly this situation often arises. There is a sentimental attitude towards the heresies of the past based on the idea that these were always liberating movements which struck off the fetters of ancient dogmas. More generally they were engaged in substituting new fetters for old ones. Sometimes they were attempts to tighten up ancient fetters by requiring a new rigor of behaviour or of belief, for example, the Donatists and the Jansenists.

The function of the Church as guardian of the faith need not be regarded as the dictation of an ancient group as to what one must believe at the present time. Rather it may be considered as the provision of a chart which will help the ordinary church-member to attain the goal of love for God and for his neighbour. That such a chart is derived in large measure from the accumulated experience and thought of the past does not in itself make the chart unlikely to be of value to the modern man. That in some respects it may need to be revised is not an unreasonable expectation; it was revised frequently and somewhat drastically in the first few centuries of the Christian Church.

One of its values may be that it can warn the Christian believer of directions of thought which may lead him astray from the goal. These need not be regarded as prohibitions but as warnings; it is the duty of the Church to tell its members that certain ways of thinking have been tried in the past and have been found to lead in directions not profitable to the spiritual life.

Much of the Athanasian Creed can be regarded as a system of such warnings. It tells the Christian believer that, if he wants to think clearly about God, and about Jesus Christ as divine, and about the Holy Spirit that came to the Apostles at Pentecost, he should not try to think of God the Father, God the Son, and God the Holy Spirit as indistinguishably one or as entirely separate. Similarly, it warns him that if he wants to think of Jesus Christ in the way that he is presented in the Gospels, he should not think of him as just God or as just man, or as God with the appearance of being a man, or as God turned into man. These are, as it were, sign-posts warning the ordinary church-member from unprofitable lines of speculation. They say, in effect: "It is of no use to think in these ways. They will only lead you into muddles and interfere with your devotional life." It remains true that a particular Christian believer may feel himself impelled to disregard the warnings and follow these old lines of speculation in the hope of finding out for himself whether they are really unprofitable.

One must, I think, consider that the warnings are more general than mere warnings as to speculative thinking. They may also be thought to refer to dangers to devotional attitudes. Distortions of devotional attitude may, for example, result from overemphasis on one person of the Trinity. Religion may be exaggeratedly Father-centred, Jesus-centred, or Spirit-centred.

A Father-centred religion was perhaps most characteristically found in England at about the eighteenth century. Its characteristic appeal was to do the will of

God and to rely on His protection. In its exaggerated form it tended to be legalistic and formal, distrustful of tenderness and of enthusiasm. It is found as one variant of religious attitude at the present time; it leads to a form of Christianity not very different in its fundamental attitudes from Judaism or Islam.

More common at the present time is a Jesus-centred religion. Its characteristic appeal is to come to Jesus, to accept him as one's personal Saviour, and to become like him. Its tendency is to sentimentality and to neglect of the sterner side of Christianity.

There is also a danger of lack of balance in a Christianity which is exaggeratedly Spirit-centred. Its appeal is to the interior life, and it may tend to ignore the Gospel history and concentrate on inner experience. It tends to enthusiasm and to neglect of tradition.

None of these types of religious attitude is to be condemned for what it asserts; all are in danger of losing something of what has been traditionally regarded as the full faith of Christianity. One may regard the Athanasian Creed as containing a warning against such lack of balance in attitude: "But the Godhead of the Father, of the Son, and of the Holy Ghost, is all one: the Glory equal, the Majesty co-eternal."

Whether as pointing out unprofitable lines of intellectual speculation or imperfect devotional attitudes, the Church cannot evade the responsibility for giving such warnings if it be true that some ways of thinking and feeling are liable to interfere with the Christian life. It is possible that the Church may decide now or in the future that some of the warning sign-posts were erected in wrong places; it may decide that, even when erected in the right places, the attached warnings were too drastic. It is obvious that the positions of the warnings were partly determined by the particular circumstances of the period during which the creeds were written. In the fourth century, the authorities of the Church were concerned with such questions as that of the Nature of Jesus Christ and of his relation to God the Father and to the Holy Spirit. Rather more than a thousand years later, about the time of the Reformation, the questions that were dividing Christians were problems of justification, of grace, and of predestination. If the creeds had been composed then, the sign-posts would have referred to such problems as these. If they had been composed at the present day, it is quite possible that the sign-posts would have been in the nature of a general warning against asking metaphysical questions about the nature of the Trinity or of Christ's divinity, on the ground that reflective thought on such topics can lead to no real knowledge but divert attention from the true goal of Christianity by producing intellectual muddles and doctrinal divisions.

Has the Church the further duty of preventing teaching which it regards as false? I have already quoted Simone Weil in her condemnation of the phrase *anathema sit*. Simone Weil, however, also said: "The function of the Church as the collective keeper of dogma is indispensable. She has the right and the duty to punish those who make a clear attack upon her within the specific range of this function by depriving them of the sacraments."[1] It is clear that she is here referring to those who teach doctrines opposed to the Church, not to those who merely believe such doctrines. That is, she is advocating disciplinary action against heresiarchs, not against heretics. The problem of tolerance of individual deviations of

[1] Weil, S., *Waiting on God* (Eng. trans.), London, 1951.

belief and that of tolerance of unorthodox teaching are two different problems. A very wide tolerance of unorthodox opinions amongst church-members does not necessitate equally wide tolerance of unorthodox teaching by its commissioned ministers.

A Church, like any other teaching body, cannot be indifferent to the activity of those of its teaching officials who teach doctrines opposed to those accepted by the Church itself. We condemn the Spanish Inquisition, for example, for its severity to those who merely believed doctrines contrary to the accepted orthodoxy of the Church, and also for the cruelty with which it punished what it regarded as false teaching. But we should not condemn it for the fact that it tried to suppress false teaching. The Church in Spain could not have been indifferent to the fact that some of its ministers were Moors and Jews who had made profession of the Christian faith without really believing it, or to the fact that some of them were teaching doctrines which were non-Christian.[1] No Church that held any system of faith could have done otherwise than deprive such ministers of their office and their church-membership. Our indignation against the cruelties of torture and burning at the stake should not blind us to the need for some sort of control of the teaching of the commissioned teachers of the Church.

Nor should we blind ourselves to the fact that there are real problems at the present day about the degree to which heretical teaching may properly be tolerated. One may sometimes hear from a pulpit in the Church of England various doctrines taught, not as private convictions of the preacher but as beliefs obligatory on all church-members. From one pulpit one may hear

[1] Turberville, A. S., *The Spanish Inquisition*, London, 1932.

that it is necessary that all Christians should believe that every word of the Bible is literally true or that no one is a Christian who has not undergone a conversion experience. From another pulpit one may hear that it is a binding necessity for all Christians that they should believe that the Blessed Virgin Mary was conceived without taint of original sin, or that they should believe that the consecrated elements in the Blessed Sacrament are no longer of the substance of bread and wine.

These are examples of the binding on of fetters which the Church of England has not bound. Those who listen to such teaching with critical and alert minds may well turn away and decide that the Christian faith is not for them. Is it reasonable that those who exercise authority in the Church should ignore the possible evil effects of such teaching because the word 'heresy' has now an unpleasant odour?

Similar problems arise even in a scientific society. In such a society there is wide tolerance of individual differences of opinion, and exclusion from membership for holding unorthodox opinions would be considered to be unreasonable and unjust. If, for example, an experimental psychologist were to be excluded from a psychological society because experimental evidence had led him to a belief in telepathy which his fellow-members did not share, there would be general agreement that this was an intolerable outrage against the freedom of scientific opinion; it could also be rightly condemned as opposed to the important aim of scientific research that it should open new fields of knowledge. Of course, deviations from accepted scientific orthodoxy have been penalised, but in scientific controversy we recognise such action to be absurd. But is the persecution of heresy really less absurd in religious controversy? May not the apparently heretical religious idea of to-day be the opening of a new field of religious knowledge which may become the orthodoxy of to-morrow?

Nevertheless, in a scientific group also there are real problems of orthodoxy and of how far heretical teaching can be tolerated. Every scientific society has a body of orthodox doctrine which it helps to hand down. It is true that over a large range of questions there is no expectation that all the members of a scientific group will think alike; indeed, diversity of belief and controversy about opinions form an important part of the object of such groups. There are, however, some questions about which there was controversy in the past but which are now regarded as settled, and these form a body of orthodox opinion which the society transmits to its members through its academic teachers. A student of physics is now taught, for example, that heat is to be thought of as motion and not as a caloric substance, as was at one time supposed. If a member of a physical society confessed to a belief in the theory of caloric, he would be regarded as eccentric, but it would not be a ground for excluding him from the society. But if a lecturer in physics taught the caloric theory as scientific orthodoxy, he would be considered to be culpably misleading his students; he would indeed be a heresiarch. One could not charge the Physics department of a university with unreasonable intolerance if he were dismissed from his lectureship. While a student would not be excluded from a Physics department because he held the caloric theory as a private opinion, he would be warned that he was wasting his time if he planned a research based on that theory.

The individual (non-teaching) member of a scientific society may also be subject to disciplinary action by the Council of the society, although they will make no inquisition into his private beliefs. If, for example, a member of a psychological society starts practising in some branch of psychological medicine in which he has no training, or if he joins a society which promotes quack psychological medicine, either action would be considered to be sufficient grounds for depriving him of his membership.

It is also the case that in a scientific society there is something to some extent corresponding to the condition of acceptance into a Church by assent to a creed. It differs in the fact that what is required is not the acceptance of any part of the orthodox teaching, but it is required that the entrant to a scientific society should accept the general aim for which the society exists. This also is a requirement of a Church before it accepts a member for baptism. Although there is no declaration of faith by an intending entrant to a scientific society, there is ordinarily a scrutiny by the Council of the society of the qualifications of the candidate. If he appears not to be genuinely concerned with the aims of the society but to wish for membership only for social or professional advantages, his application for membership is likely to be rejected. In the same way a Church must make some examination of the qualifications of an intending entrant, whether or not the traditional way of doing it by seeing whether he assents to the Apostles' Creed is an adequate method for this purpose.

Chapter Seven

PRACTICAL PROBLEMS OF AUTHORITY IN MATTERS OF BELIEF

IT is reasonable to suggest that a Church can best exercise its function as guardian of the faith if it is clear as to what are the elements of faith it has the duty of guarding. There are a variety of reasons for a considerable lack of clarity in this matter among some branches of the Church at the present time. The main factor is, I think, that there has been increasing tolerance in practice of diversity of belief which has not been accompanied by any revision of authoritative formulae expressing an intolerant attitude towards such diversity. Thus there has developed an increasing divergence between theory and practice in this matter. I shall limit my discussion to the situation as it has developed in the Church of England since this is the aspect of the problem that I know best, but I think that the same contradiction between theory and practice is to be found in other reformed Churches.

Beliefs may be classed in various categories according to the degree to which acceptance of them is required by a church-member. We may distinguish the following traditionally recognised categories of belief:

(i) *Obligatory beliefs*, which are taught as true by the Church and which every church-member is required to believe as a condition of his membership. Complementary to these are *prohibited beliefs*, which the Church teaches to be false and assent to which by a church-member would be regarded as a ground for excluding him from the Church or (in the old days) for punishing him as a heretic.

(ii) *Permitted beliefs*, which may be either accepted or rejected by a church-member since the Church has made no authoritative pronouncement on their truth or falsity. For example, the Roman Catholic is permitted to believe or disbelieve any story of a miracle performed by a saint other than those recorded in Scripture, the member of the Church of England is permitted to believe or to disbelieve that the body of the Blessed Virgin Mary was taken up into Heaven, or that every word of the Bible is literally true. In neither of these cases would it be proper for a commissioned teacher of the Church to teach that the belief in question is an obligatory belief or that it is a prohibited belief.

(iii) *Indifferent beliefs*, which are about matters on which the Church has no authority to decide whether they are true or false. These include all beliefs about secular history and about the matters dealt with in the descriptive and theoretical sciences. It is sometimes difficult to draw a sharp line between matters that belong entirely to the secular field and those that have religious significance, but there is now general agreement that there is a field of secular matters of opinion in which no religious authority can properly exercise authority either in determining what should be believed or what may be taught. We are warned by the history of the condemnation of Galileo and the ecclesiastical pronouncements on Darwin's theory of evolution of the danger of mistaking secular opinions for religious beliefs.

The situation with respect to authority in matters of

belief is clear in the Church of Rome. Belief in a large number of dogmas is obligatory; there are other religious opinions which the individual member of the Roman Church is free either to accept or to reject, and he is, of course, free to accept or reject beliefs belonging to the indifferent category. The general tendency of development has been to increase the first class of beliefs at the expense of the second, and beliefs which were once permitted later become obligatory. The doctrine of the bodily assumption of the Blessed Virgin Mary, for example, which was at one time a permitted opinion, has now become an obligatory belief. Clarity as to what is or is not to be believed is here achieved at the cost of loss of intellectual freedom, and, as it appears to protestant religious bodies, at the further cost of requiring belief in much that is of uncertain truth or of little importance.

For this reason those members of reformed Churches who are aware of the inconveniences resulting from the lack of clarity as to what their members are required to believe are generally unwilling to follow Rome in the methods of achieving clarity. It is not necessary for clarity that obligatory beliefs should be maximised; it is only necessary that there should be a clear distinction between beliefs that are and those that are not obligatory. Intellectual freedom and tolerance are best achieved if the class of obligatory beliefs is reduced to a minimum and includes only those fundamental beliefs which are essential to the Christian faith. None would doubt, for example, that belief in God is such a fundamental belief. It is generally agreed also that belief in the divinity of Jesus Christ is a fundamental belief of Christianity, although it is a belief rejected by many devout and pious persons. There seems less reason for regarding as fundamental beliefs obligatory on all members of the Church such statements as that Jesus Christ was born of the Virgin Mary or that he descended into hell. These may be true, and it may be better that the individual member of the Church should believe them. There seems no sufficient reason for regarding them as obligatory in the sense that disbelief in them should automatically cut off the unbeliever from the Christian fellowship.

It may, of course, be argued that rejection of any doctrine taught as true by the Church implies rebellion against the authority of the Church and that this rebellion in itself is a ground for exclusion from the Church, whether the belief rejected is an important or an unimportant one. This is a reasonable argument if the Church is regarded as infallible. If, however, it is not part of our faith in the Church of England that the Church of England cannot err, the argument lacks an essential premiss. Since the reformers believed that the Church of England was gravely in error on many points of doctrine before the Reformation, they could not reasonably have claimed, and did not in fact claim, that it became infallible after the Reformation.

At the time of the Reformation, the Church of England rejected as unjustified accretions to the original Christian faith many of the beliefs which were previously regarded as obligatory. There appears, however, to have been no intention of reducing the burden of obligatory belief. The new standard of doctrine contained in the Articles of Religion which have now become thirty-nine in number was clearly intended to be obligatory in the sense that all members of the Church of England were expected to believe them although the ordinary layman was not required to express his assent to them. That he was expected to believe them is clear from the Declaration of King Charles I which is still printed at their head: "requiring all Our loving Subjects to continue in the uniform Profession thereof, and prohibiting the least difference from the said Articles". In practice, a great deal of this system of belief is now treated as not obligatory but permitted; deviations are tolerated although the written rules as to belief have remained unchanged.

The enquirer who turns to the prayer-book to discover what he would be expected to believe if he became a member of the Church finds that he is required to believe in the Creeds and also in the Thirty-nine Articles of Religion. The obligatory character of assent to the Creeds is made clear in Article VIII, which says: "The Three Creeds, *Nicene* Creed, *Athanasius's* Creed, and that which is called the *Apostles'* Creed ought thoroughly to be received and believed. . . ." The expectation that he will also believe the Articles themselves is clearly indicated by the passage from the Declaration already quoted. Later he will find a more drastic prohibition of public criticism or discussion of the Articles: "That if any public Reader in either of Our Universities, or any Head or Master of a College, or any other person respectively in either of them, shall affix any new sense to any Article, or shall publicly read, determine, or hold any publick Disputation . . . the Offenders shall be liable to Our displeasure. . . . And We will see that there shall be due Execution upon them." At the end of the preceding paragraph, he will note that it is not permissible to draw aside any Article or to make his own interpretation of it, but that he must "submit to it in the plain and full meaning thereof" and "take it in the literal and grammatical sense".

If he examines carefully the content of the Articles, he will find that they are of widely different kinds. Some reaffirm the traditional doctrines of the Catholic Church; some reflect the attitudes of sixteenth-century divines to the religious controversies of the Reformation period. Generally accepted opinions within the Church of England have often moved far from the Articles of the latter kind. For example, in the report of the Commission on Doctrine, we find: "the crudity . . . of some mediaeval conceptions of Purgatory does not rule out the essential idea of a phase of progressive growth and, it may be, of needed purification of the soul after death".[1] This suggests that a latitude of opinion on this subject is now tolerated which was not intended by Article XXII: "The Romish Doctrine concerning Purgatory . . . is a fond thing vainly invented, and grounded upon no warranty of Scripture, but rather repugnant to the word of God." It is true that one may make the opinion consistent with the Article by saying that what is condemned in the Article is not any doctrine of purgatory but only the Romish doctrine concerning purgatory, but this is surely turning aside the meaning of the Article in the manner condemned in the Declaration and not submitting to it in the plain and full meaning thereof.

In Article XIII *Of Works before Justification*, we are told: "Works done before the grace of Christ . . . are not pleasant to God . . . yea rather . . . we doubt not but they have the nature of sins." Again adopting, as

---

[1] The Commission on Christian Doctrine appointed by the Archbishops of Canterbury and York, *Doctrine in the Church of England*, London, 1938.

G

we are required to do, the plain meaning of this Article, it seems to mean that the virtues of those outside the Christian fold are sins: that Socrates and Marcus Aurelius Antoninus were guilty of sin by living more in accordance with the Christian pattern of life than do most professing Christians. This is an arguable position, but it would generally be rejected as false; certainly it is not to be considered to be an obligatory belief.

In contrast with the rigid system of requirements as to belief presented in the Articles and the Declaration, there is great latitude in practice. If I should earn the Royal displeasure and the due execution referred to in the Declaration for having expressed disagreement with some of the Articles, I should find myself one of a great company including most Divinity Professors and many Bishops. In practice, the Declaration is obsolete now and is not taken seriously. Why, then, does it still appear in the prayer-book? It does not disturb members of the Church of England since they do not commonly read either it or the Articles. It may be a serious obstacle to those who are wishing to join a Christian Church and who hope to find in the Church of England a body to whose doctrinal system they can honestly assent.

One may be somewhat blinded as to the reality of the divergence between theory and practice in the Church of England with respect to requirements of belief by a habit of talking as if our tolerance in practice were reflected in our written rules about belief. I have read, for example, that the Church of England does not require conformity to any particular standard of belief, and that the Thirty-nine Articles of Religion have been rendered obsolete by the publication of the report of the Commission on Christian Doctrine appointed by the Archbishops of Canterbury and York in 1922.[1] This may describe the recognised practice, but it is contrary to written rules about conformity of belief as printed in the prayer-book. The Commission on Doctrine was merely an advisory body whose recommendations have no authority until they have been translated into regulations by the Church of England.

It has also increasingly been argued in recent years that the Articles have no plain meaning, but, on the contrary, were worded so ambiguously as to admit of a wide variety of interpretations. This may be the case, but in asserting that it is so, we are plainly going against the Declaration since a requirement to submit to the "plain and full meaning" of each Article implies that it has a plain and full meaning. If, in practice, we deny this implication, this too is a divergence between our practice and the rules.

It is true that there was some reduction of the divergence between theory and practice when in 1865, candidates for holy orders were required only to assert their belief that the doctrine of the Church of England set forth in the Articles was agreeable to the Word of God. This was intended to imply that they assented to the general sense of the Articles and not necessarily to all of their details. This, however, goes a very small way towards bridging the gap, which also has considerably widened since 1865.

The honest enquirer who wants to find out what he is expected to believe if he joins the Church of England will not feel himself concerned with the form of assent

[1] The Commission on Christian Doctrine appointed by the Archbishops of Canterbury and York, *Doctrine in the Church of England*, London, 1938.

required from the clergy, nor will he study the text-books on the Articles which discuss their ambiguities and their intended comprehensiveness. He will go to the prayer-book, and there he will find the Declaration, which tells him unambiguously the extent to which he is required to believe what is stated in the Articles.

Such an enquirer will be little helped by someone who tells him: "You need not bother about the Declaration or the Articles since they are no longer taken seriously." He may reply that that is what troubles him. He feels it to be an offence against his intellectual integrity to accept an obligation of belief which he is not supposed to take seriously.

The situation is indeed rather like that sometimes found in a public school where new boys find a complicated system of rules, all of which they begin, in their innocence, to try to keep. It is only when they have been at school for a term or two that they pick up its traditions well enough to know which of its rules they are really expected to keep and which they may break with impunity. This situation should not occur in a religious body. No obligations should appear to be imposed on its members which in practice are not imposed.

This is no doubt merely a transitional situation. Where change is taking place it may easily happen that behaviour changes more rapidly than do the written rules which govern behaviour. There are obvious reasons why in a religious organisation this should be the case since there are strong social forces in the direction of resisting change and these may be more effective in keeping the rules constant than in preserving the practice unchanged. Yet the situation is one of tension which cannot be allowed to continue indefinitely. It can be resolved by revising our rules as to belief in order to make them conform to the very widely tolerant practice, or by the exercise of disciplinary action to make practice within the Church of England conform to our existing rules. It is likely that neither of these things will happen altogether but that there will be modification of both rules and practice in such a way as to produce convergence.

Their present divergence has, of course, historical roots. The Reformation divines inherited a tradition that whatever was pronounced as true by a Church must be believed by all its members, and they did not question that tradition. They themselves, moreover, made drastic changes with respect to the official beliefs of their Church, but they made no provision for further change. Their conviction that the Church of Rome had erred did not apparently lead them to consider the possibility that they might also be judged by later ages to have erred in some respects. Whatever solution may be adopted for resolving our present divergence between theory and practice in respect to requirements of belief must not again be supposed to be a final one. Provision must be made for new adjustments in future times.

If there is less difference between theory and practice with respect to belief in the Creeds than with respect to belief in the Articles of Religion, the situation is by no means clear even here. There is a widespread opinion that members of the Anglican Church are expected to believe all of the Apostles' and Nicene Creeds while they are not similarly bound to believe all of the Athanasian Creed. There is, however, no authoritative pronouncement endorsing this distinction, while the Article already quoted (No. VIII) is an unabrogated authoritative pronouncement against it. In practice, indeed, the freedom is much wider. Denial of particular statements even in the Apostles' Creed may not prevent a clergyman from holding high office in the Church, although assent to the whole of the Apostles' Creed is, in the Church of England, required by any unbaptised entrant into the Church at his baptismal service.

Nor would it seem to be a satisfactory solution of the problem of what is to be regarded as obligatory in Christian belief to say that all propositions contained in the creeds should be obligatory and all other propositions of Christian belief merely permitted. One may have great reverence for the ancient creeds and yet recognise that their statements go well beyond a reasonable minimum of obligatory belief. The original baptismal professions out of which the creeds grew were, no doubt, statements of what was regarded as the minimum of Christian belief, but the creeds developed as formulae for the exclusion of heretical beliefs, and many of their statements are not affirmations of fundamental Christian experiences but of theological propositions derived from these. If it is agreed that a member of the Church must acknowledge that Jesus is God, it does not appear to be equally necessary that he should affirm that he was "of one substance with the Father" or that he was "of a reasonable soul and human flesh subsisting". These statements may be meaningful and true (or at least as much so as the limitations of language as a means of expressing the inexpressible allows them to be) and yet they remain ways of attempting to make precise the implications of the fundamental statement that Jesus is God. They are themselves statements of a different order from that, and their acceptance may be considered to be of relatively secondary importance.

Also the Apostles' Creed contains statements of a historical order: "Born of the Virgin Mary, Suffered under Pontius Pilate, Was crucified, dead, and buried". These may be considered to be true without also being considered to be of the same fundamental importance as "I believe in God the Father Almighty . . . and in Jesus Christ his only Son our Lord". Belief that these historical statements are true does not imply that if they were proved to be false there would remain no foundation for the fundamental affirmations of the Christian religion. Let us suppose, for example, that a scholar was convinced as a result of his researches that the Procurator at the time of the crucifixion was not Pontius Pilate but his successor. It would not be considered that this scholar had lost his Christian faith, although it might be thought that he was mistaken. His mistake would be of a wholly different order from that involved if his researches had led him to believe that Jesus Christ was not God.

I would suggest that the most hopeful direction in which tolerance of individual deviations in belief may be developed without abrogation of the function of the Church as the guardian of traditional teaching is to recognise that a belief may be part of the true teaching of the Church and yet that the individual church-member need not regard himself as obliged to assent to it. Such a belief would differ from a *permitted* belief in the fact that the Church does assert its truth; it would differ from an *obligatory* belief in the fact that the Church does not regard assent to it as of such import ance that failure to assent is inconsistent with continued church - membership or with admission to church-membership. This would be to add a fourth category of beliefs to the three listed on p. 92 f., a category which may be called that of *orthodox non-essential* beliefs. I would suggest further that this class should be a large one and that the class of obligatory beliefs should be very small.

The idea that an item of belief might be orthodox and yet non-obligatory would have been equally unacceptable in the fourth and following centuries when the creeds were being constructed and in the sixteenth century when the Reformation took place. This was one of the psychological factors in the development and continuance of religious intolerance. When a doctrine was defined as true, it was also regarded as necessary that every church-member should believe it; no difference in this respect was made between doctrines of different degrees of importance.

When, for example, the controversy took place between the Arians and their opponents, it was not unreasonable to regard the issue as so vital to Christian belief that one who refused to accept the orthodox doctrine was excommunicated. Whether or not it was right to make the acceptance of the anti-Arian view obligatory on all church-members, it was certainly not unreasonable.

But when the Churches of the East and the West were divided on the question of whether one should say that "the Holy Ghost proceeded from the Father" or that "the Holy Ghost proceeded from the Father and the Son", it cannot reasonably be maintained that this was a vital issue. The Church might well have decided to put whatever solution was adopted into the category of orthodox non-essential beliefs if such a category had been recognised. This would have meant that they said in effect: so-and-so is the right way of saying it, but it will make no difference to your Christian life or to your devotions whether you use the one formula or the other, so the question of which you use is of no importance; it is of real importance that you should not offend against charity by condemning those to whom the other formula seems better. There were, of course, social and psychological reasons why this solution could not have been adopted at that time; I do not think that there is any reason for supposing that it would not have been the right solution.

Let us consider a problem belonging more to our own time. A man may sincerely believe in the divinity of our Lord Jesus Christ and yet find himself unable to believe in the Virgin Birth of Jesus. Is that to be a tolerated opinion, or should it automatically exclude the person holding it from membership of the Church and from participation in the sacraments? Alternatively, ought we to say that since many scholars of the present day do not believe in the doctrine of the Virgin Birth, this belief should not be regarded as part of the faith of the Church? Many people would be inclined to reject both of these solutions. The Virgin Birth is part of the traditional teaching of the Church; to suggest that it should not be regarded as an obligatory doctrine is not to suggest that it is not true. We may consider that it is not an essential doctrine because its importance lies not in itself but in its function as safeguarding doctrine for the more important doctrine of the Incarnation. The solution of the difficulty might be that belief in the Virgin Birth was regarded as an orthodox non-essential belief. This would mean that the Church affirmed it as true but did not require its acceptance as a condition for church-membership.

Let us suppose that a man holding this unorthodox opinion was not baptised as a child and wishes to be baptised and to become a member of the Church of England. He knows that members of that Church and even some holding high office in it share his view. If he were in any doubt about the fact that this is a tolerated opinion in practice, he would find that it was held by some of the scholars and theologians who formed the Archbishops' Commission on Doctrine in the Church of England. He may read in their report: "There are, however, some among us who hold that a full belief in the historical Incarnation is more consistent with the supposition that our Lord's birth took place under the normal conditions of human generation. In their minds the notion of a Virgin Birth tends to mar the completeness of the belief that in the Incarnation God revealed Himself at every point in and through human nature" (p. 82).[1]

Yet although he knows that his doctrinal position is one that in practice is recognised as a permitted one in the Church of England, he cannot be baptised in an Anglican church unless he is willing to perjure himself in that solemn service by answering "All this I steadfastly believe" to the recital of the Apostles' Creed, which includes the clause "And that he was conceived by the Holy Ghost; born of the Virgin Mary".

It may, of course, be maintained that assent to the doctrine of the Virgin Birth is part of the essential minimum of belief obligatory on every member of the Church; in that case it is wrong that in practice those holding office in the Church of England should be

[1] The Commission on Christian Doctrine appointed by the Archbishops of Canterbury and York, *Doctrine in the Church of England*, London, 1938.

permitted to deny this doctrine. If, on the other hand, it be held that this doctrine, though true, is not part of the essential minimum of belief, it is wrong that one not believing it should find himself excluded from baptism.

If this belief is considered to be an orthodox non-essential belief, the Apostles' Creed cannot be regarded as a suitable baptismal formula. One might for this purpose substitute a simpler affirmation of belief containing only those statements assent to which is regarded by the Church as essential for baptism. Such a minimal profession of belief is, in fact, used in the baptismal service of the Church of Rome, where the candidate for baptism is required to respond "I do believe" to each of the following questions: "Dost thou believe in God the Father Almighty, Creator of heaven and earth?", "Dost thou believe in Jesus Christ, his only begotten Son, our Lord, who was born, who suffered?", and "Dost thou also believe in the Holy Ghost, the holy Catholic Church, the communion of saints, the forgiveness of sins, the resurrection of the body and life everlasting?"[1].

This is not, of course, a full statement of the beliefs which are now regarded as obligatory in the Church of Rome. It may be a relic of a much earlier time when this was all that was regarded as essential for the candidate for baptism to assent to. If the Church of England decided to extend in theory the tolerance of this particular doctrinal deviation which it already extends in practice, some such formula of assent in baptism would be more suitable than the present use of the Apostles' Creed. It would not, of course, include all that the Church teaches as true. No baptismal

[1] Fleury, A., S.J., *The Missal Explained* (Eng. trans.), London, 1916.

formula is meant to do that; certainly not the Apostles' Creed. A baptismal formula is required to contain the minimum essentials of belief; the full teaching will always be much more.

If such a Christian belief as that in the Virgin Birth were regarded as non-obligatory, this would not imply that it is treated as not true or as not part of the orthodox teaching of the Catholic Church. Those who hold the orthodox view may indeed hope that the individual who is admitted to the Communion of the Church in spite of holding unorthodox opinions may come to hold the orthodox opinion as a result of his experience within the Church. One may think that he is wrong in his opinions and regret the wrongness of his opinions without thinking that it should automatically exclude him from the Christian fellowship.

I have taken the Virgin Birth as an example of a belief which might be treated as not obligatory but as belonging to the category of orthodox non-essential beliefs because this is a matter of current controversy. There are many other beliefs about which similar questions might be asked. Since delivering these lectures, a book by Simone Weil has been published in which she asks of many other beliefs whether they are prohibited beliefs or whether they could be regarded as permitted even though the general consensus of opinion in the Church is against them.[1] She suggests, for example, that in the period several centuries before Christ the Hebrew Scriptures show less understanding of the nature of God than the religious literature of India, Egypt, Greece, and China. She suggests that idolatory also may have been a road to God. She suggests that the Eleusinian mysteries and those of

[1] Weil, Simone, *Letter to a Priest* (Eng. trans.), London, 1953.

Osiris may have been real sacraments. She suggests that every time a man has, with a pure heart, called upon Osiris, Dionysus, Krishna, Buddha, the Tao, etc., the Son of God has answered him by sending the Holy Spirit.

With the increasing awareness amongst Christians of the religious character of non-Christian faiths, questions of this kind will be increasingly asked. The Church may condemn such opinions as wholly prohibited, it may treat them as permitted opinions whether or not it also regards them as false opinions. It is important that ecclesiastical authority should not automatically treat them as prohibited merely because they are new. It is also important that no branch of the Church should increase bewilderment as to obligations of belief by condemning them as prohibited in theory while in practice tolerating them as permitted.

CHAPTER EIGHT

INTELLECTUAL EXPLORATION

R ELIGIOUS dogmas are generally regarded as warning-
notices against the exploration of certain lines of
thought. There may, however, be more than one kind
of warning-notice. One might, in walking through a
wood, see a notice at the entrance to a footpath:
"This route is not advised since the track is boggy",
or one might see a notice: "Keep out". The ordinary
behaviour-response in both cases will be to avoid the
footpath, but with the important difference that in the
first case the walker can go along the path if he likes
and can discover for himself that it is too muddy to
walk along, while in the second he suffers the frustrating
experience of being prohibited from doing so.

One may interpret the negative implications of
religious doctrines in either of these senses; I suggest
that it is better that they should be interpreted in the
first sense, even although this is a departure from
tradition. It is clear that the second sense was what
was meant in the days of religious persecution. To
walk along the paths of intellectual speculation not
approved by the Church was the sin of heresy. If one
persisted in such exploration after warning, or if one
strayed into such paths again after having once
renounced one's heresy, the penalty might be death by
burning.

No doubt these measures kept many people away
from such forbidden paths and produced a high average
level of verbal assent to the orthodox doctrines, but at a

heavy price. Part of the price must have been that much of the assent was at a superficial level. Freedom to explore other paths may be the way to attain fuller understanding of the approved paths. It is true that one who is free to wander may never come back to the approved paths; that is a risk that must be taken by the religious explorer. The price of freedom is that one has freedom also to make mistakes; the price of intellectual bondage is that assent remains at a superficial level.

If a psychologist wants to teach a rat to run through a maze he will not do so by stopping up all the blind alleys so that the rat can follow only the one right path which is left open to him. On the contrary, he lets the rat explore the blind alleys and find out for himself which is the right path to the goal. No doubt we generally begin by receiving religious doctrines passively as a child learns the multiplication tables passively. But if the child is to attain real understanding of numerical relationships it must be by advancing beyond this stage of passive acceptance and exploring various ways of combining and relating numbers, wrong ways as well as right, so that he can with full insight reject the wrong and accept the right ones. In the same way, religious doctrines, originally received passively, attain for the believer life and reality by his subsequent exploration of the country to which they refer.

I do not wish to suggest that all people are called upon to make intellectual explorations in matters of religion. Some may find their way to God by the method of unquestioning acceptance and simple faith. Some, however, are led to criticise and enquire, and I suggest that it should not be the function of religious dogma to prohibit such enquiry but rather to enable the modern enquirer to know what conclusions have been reached in the past by devout and reasonable men who have undertaken similar enquiries. He is free to follow other paths than those they took, but he would be unwise if he ignored their findings.

If part of the purpose of intellectual exploration of religious ideas is to enrich understanding of religious truths, it may be considered that even the central affirmation of religious faith, "I believe in God", may be profitably accompanied by the exploration of the possibility that this affirmation may be wrong. There is also the possibility that the world as described by history and science is all that there is: that we are sentient organisms produced accidentally by a blind process of organic evolution, that the universe has no purpose and goes on for ever, new nebulae condensing and receding from one another with life occasionally evolving on planets that happen to have the right temperature and atmosphere, and that our consciousness is merely an accidental consequence of the complexity of our nervous systems and ceases for ever with our bodily death. That is possible, but the religious man does not think that it is true. His belief in God and immortality is a choice rejecting that possibility, a choice which may have been made on rational grounds and which may be the right choice, but we cannot be certain that it is so. The other possibility remains and our religious faith will be more firmly based if we do not refuse to consider the other possibility but squarely face it.

In the past, religious teachers have generally been inclined to discourage such lines of thought as leading to the danger of loss of religious faith or at best to uncertainty in holding it. These are, of course, dangers, but there are also gains to faith which, I think, out-weigh the dangers. First, a clear recognition of the truth of the possibility of the opposite of what one believes is an attitude favourable to tolerance of those who hold the opposite opinion. Such an intellectual operation on the part of the mediaeval persecutors would have removed some of the blackest pages from ecclesiastical history. Secondly, it may bring a height-ened awareness of the truths of religion. A man will have a more solid understanding of what it means to say "I believe in God" if he has thought out the possibility and implications of the opposite assertion "I believe in no God". Thirdly, it may result in religious faith being more firmly grounded. The man who has never considered the possibility of the opposite is in a somewhat precarious state of balance which may be upset by any presentation in speech or writing of the case against religious belief. We may notice that when heresy was most sternly repressed it was also necessary to prohibit the faithful from reading heretical books. They were treated like people who had lost their immunity to infection and must therefore be protected against any contact with infectious disease. The fear underlying this prohibition was probably well founded, but the modern man cannot be so protected from con-tact with anti-religious systems of thought. He must have the immunity provided by having thought out the case against religion as fully as possible.

At one time it was supposed that speculative thought could provide a coercive case for the acceptance of the religious interpretation of the universe. This opinion is now generally rejected by philosophers. Even if it were accepted, it would not follow that every

H

reasonable person would be compelled to believe by considering arguments which were logically adequate to support belief, since the fact that an argument is logically incontrovertible does not imply that it is psychologically adequate to create belief. The psychological inadequacy of the traditional arguments for the existence of God can be easily observed. I well remember the chill I felt when I first heard the ontological argument for the existence of God. It sounded to me like a mere verbal trick, and the chill came from the fear that it was ultimately on such a hollow foundation that religious faith must rest.

If we renounce the hope of finding a logically coercive proof of the truth of a religious explanation of the universe, we must ask on what intellectual foundation religious faith does rest. It seems to be widely assumed, both by religious believers and by unbelievers, that either there is a logically incontrovertible proof of the religious position or else religious belief has no rational foundation. Some of those who accept this dilemma would maintain that religious belief has no rational basis and yet that we are justified in accepting it on other than rational grounds. Thus William James says: "Our passional natures not only lawfully may, but must decide an option between propositions, whenever it is a genuine option that cannot by its nature be decided on intellectual grounds."[1] That, I think, is a dangerous line of defence for religious belief. If nothing but our passional natures determined our acceptance of religious belief, the intellectual foundations of our faith would be weak indeed. It would seem preferable to accept the uncompromising rationalism of Freud:

[1] James, W., "The Will to Believe", *Selected Papers on Philosophy*, London, 1917 (first published 1896).

"Ignorance is ignorance; no right to believe anything is derived from it."[1]

This alternative of either a coercive intellectual proof of the truth of religion or the adoption of faith on wholly irrational grounds does not, however, exhaust the possibilities. It assumes that the only rational grounds on which religious belief may be accepted are intellectual processes of the same kind as those used in proving a mathematical proposition. They may, however, be regarded in another way, as an empirical judgment based on a weighing of evidence similar to that made by a jury when deciding on a verdict. The acceptance of a belief in God and in a spiritual world may be considered to be neither an insight into a necessity of thought nor an emotional decision without rational foundation but an act of faith whose rational foundation is a judgment based on a consideration of all the available evidence.

Regarded not as coercive proofs but as part of the evidence, the traditional arguments for the existence of God cannot be so lightly dismissed as they commonly are by those who judge them as if they were mathematical proofs. The argument from design, for example, may be important if it is considered as an empirical argument which, by its nature as an empirical argument, cannot provide a certain conclusion. Our opinion as to the being and nature of God is rightly founded to some extent on our conviction as to whether there is a pattern and design in the universe and as to what sort of pattern and design are to be found there. This, however, is part of a process of weighing the evidence and forming a judgment. To be a genuinely rational process it must be the resultant of the consideration of different

[1] Freud, S., *The Future of an Illusion* (Eng. trans.), London, 1928.

H*

lines of evidence; we must not only consider with Paley the structure of the human eye[1] but also with Sherrington the adaptation of the liver fluke and the malarial protozoon to inflict pain and disease on their hosts.[2] Like other empirical judgments of everyday life, this is a matter in which some of the evidence may seem to point one way and some another, and our task is to weigh the evidence and make the best judgment we can. There are, of course, other kinds of evidence to consider: that derived from our experience of beauty and ugliness, of moral good and evil, and also the body of specifically religious experiences of ourselves and the more profound experiences of the mystics and saints. It is not absurd to look for evidence from states of intuition and trance; these may be conditions in which realities are perceived more clearly than in normal psychological states. Certainly we must also consider that the mystic may be mistaken in reporting his experiences of spiritual realities, but we must not omit to consider that he may be right in claiming that he has direct knowledge of a region of spiritual reality of which we at best have only a dim awareness.

We have considerable empirical grounds for making a judgment, but no empirical judgment can be certain. We may be wrong and it may be better, for reasons suggested above, that we should be clearly aware that our judgment may be wrong. It is important, however, that this recognition of uncertainty should not be allowed to make us half-hearted in action. The verdict of the jury in a criminal case is "guilty" or "not guilty", and the action dictated by the verdict is carried out completely whether it is punishment or

[1] Paley, W., *Natural Theology*, London, 1802.
[2] Sherrington, C., *Man on his Nature*, London, 1940.

acquittal. In the same way, if our judgment is for the religious interpretation of the universe, our duty is to love God with all our heart and soul, and our neighbour as ourself. The thought that our choice may be based on an illusion must not make us half-hearted in our religious action.

At this point, however, we are met by the psychological criticism of religious belief which seeks to undermine the possibility of a sound judgment. On this matter, it is said, our judgment is in no way to be relied on since our emotions are too deeply involved in the answer. We cannot bear the thought of a purposeless universe in which we are merely accidental incidents, and the process of belief determination by wish-fulfilment creates in us the conviction that there is a God and an Eternal life which will give us security now and hereafter. This is the line of thought developed by Freud in his book *The Future of an Illusion*.[1]

It is sometimes supposed by religious apologists who have read no more of Freud's book than its title that his argument was that since religion was based on a system of wishes it must be false. Freud was not so naïve as to suppose this. His argument was a more serious one: that there is no real reason for supposing that religious beliefs are true since they are not verifiable, and no one would be so frivolous as to maintain belief in a system of thought with so little justification in any other field. He considered that our reason for this intellectually irresponsible attitude towards religion was that the wishes it fulfilled were too urgent to allow us to realise how flimsy was the basis on which its beliefs were founded.

But it remains true that, although the fact that

[1] Freud, S., *The Future of an Illusion* (Eng. trans.), London, 1928.

religious beliefs may be fulfilments of wishes is a good reason for distrusting our judgment about their truth, it is not in itself a ground for judging one way or the other. This is an additional reason for considering that perhaps we may be wrong, but it is not a reason for not making the best judgment we can. We should be aware of the emotional forces which may influence our judgment and try to allow for those forces in making our judgment. The judgment in favour of a religious interpretation may still be the right one. Nor should we neglect the fact that there may also be emotional forces acting in the other direction. Some people find the conceptions of a universe limited to the physical and of a conscious life terminated by the death of the body a more comfortable system of ideas than that which includes a spiritual world and a responsibility for our actions which extends beyond the grave.

The possibility of the determination of belief by wish-fulfilment has further implications. It should make us distrustful of the modern tendency to select our system of religious beliefs so that it shall correspond with how we should like things to be here and hereafter. There were less comfortable elements in the religious faith of earlier centuries: judgment and hell and the idea of the majesty of God as well as of his love. The modern religious believer has tended to prune out such uncomfortable thoughts from his system of beliefs. Sometimes he may be right, but he is in danger of making his remaining religious ideas a sort of dream world in which he puts what he likes and discards what he does not like. There is plainly no certainty that this principle of selection is a reliable guide for discriminating the true from the false.

That the person holding a belief should consider the

possibility of its opposite is a mental exercise which may be profitable to the unbeliever as well as to the religious believer. It is perhaps unusual now to find an intellectually alert religious believer who has not at some time considered the possibility that his system of religious beliefs may be a delusion. It is, however, not uncommon to find intelligent unbelievers who are unable to consider the possibility that the religious system of ideas may be true. This indeed seems to be a weakness of the position taken by Freud.[1] His basic argument is that in any defence of religious faith the religious person is arguing frivolously; in his heart he knows very well that it is all a fairy-tale and that the universe revealed by scientific enquiry is the only reality. This amounts to saying that the possibility of the religious interpretation must be regarded as excluded from the beginning.

A clear-sighted religious unbelief must face the possibility that the religious interpretation of the universe may be the true one. It is possible that the long development of the galaxies and the process of organic evolution on our own planet are not blind and purposeless happenings but have as their end a spiritual purpose. It might even be that their whole purpose was to create one planet on which the drama of redemption might take place through the Incarnation of the Son of God. The unbeliever may feel that the size of the universe makes such an idea inconceivable, but this is plainly not a logical argument but a statement of a psychological difficulty of belief. One can give no reasonable answer to the question as to what size the universe would have to be if the religious interpretation were the true one; it might be large or small. Further-

[1] Freud, S., *The Future of an Illusion* (Eng. trans.), London, 1928.

more, one must not exclude the possibility that if the religious interpretation of the universe is the true one, the spiritual plan may be something very much more extensive than that part of it concerned with our own planet.

The demonstration of the possibility of the religious explanation must be, I think, the first task of religious apologetics at the present time. It is only the first step, and it does not in itself take one very far on the road to religious faith. It provides an essential foundation on which a structure of religious faith may be built. It is one of the characteristics of the intellectual situation in our times that this foundation is often lacking; it is often an unexamined axiom of the modern thinker that any religious system is a mere fairy-tale, belief in which is an anachronism.

If the spiritual world is accepted as a reality, it must, of course, not be thought of as a shadowy spirit-world lying behind our more real world of sensible things. If we are born for an eternal destiny, that destiny is not less real than our life here; if God exists, his reality is not less than that of physical objects, the working of his grace not less real than physical causation. The religious point of view implies that this is the system of realities for which we were born and towards which our action must be directed, and that the world of external objects and the scientific investigation of it are important primarily as means of revealing to us the glory of God.

INDEX

AUTHORITY & FREEDOM

ROBERT H. THOULESS.

200.1